Endorsements

I have known Pastor Marsha Mansour for over twenty years now. I have worked side by side with her in ministry and have witnessed her gift of leadership at work. She has the unique ability to love people as Jesus did, full of grace and truth. Marsha knows when to lead people in grace and mercy and when to speak and stand for the truth in love. This leadership style is not a science that is gained from a theological education but is an art mastered through life experience in the trenches with people. I highly recommend this book because of the depth of leadership experience and wisdom that personifies the author. May the Lord open the eyes of your heart to see leading like Jesus in a new, profound way.

—Walter E Nistorenko
Lead Pastor, Abundant Life Church, Seaville, NJ
Presbyter (Southern Section of the NJ Ministry Network)

Marsha Mansour has certainly been a living example of courage in her personal and ministry life. She walks in boldness and faith in every area! In her first book, *The Courage to Live*, she speaks confidence to the reader to live and walk with courage. Marsha is a born leader, and those skills are exemplified in the way she leads people by walking with them and leaves them wanting more. From the moment you meet her, you know that she is all about Jesus and building the Kingdom His way. There are so many leaders who know the principles of leadership but have difficulty carrying them out. Marsha not only knows the principles, but she lives them as well. *The Courage to Lead* is a leadership must-read!

—Nancy Tonnessen
Pastor of Deaf Ministries at Evangel Church, Scotch Plains, NJ
Secretary for the National Deaf Culture Fellowship
(Assemblies of God)

Some leaders are worth only a dime a dozen. That's a sad commentary! Too many lack expertise, experience, and passion. Marsha Mansour lives in contrast to the pack of ordinary or mediocre leaders. She has worked hard to develop her leadership skills, has a good track of experience, and attacks both life and ministry with a radical passion! When Marsha enters the room, you know she is present, and when she leaves, there is a definite vacuum. She is a unique leader, and her words are dependable. Enjoy the energy of her presentation as displayed within the cover of this, her latest book!

—Rev. Carl Colletti
Assemblies of God New Jersey District Superintendent,
1998–2018

Leadership requires courage. Marsha's life and ministry has embodied this principle. I have had a front-row seat to witness her courageous leadership in action over the last eleven years. The greatest testament of Marsha's leadership is found in those she has personally influenced and mentored. She creates leaders who create leaders. You will be blessed by the principles and insights in this book. They come from a lifetime of learning in the trenches and trials of ministry. May this book help you to become the leader God has called and created you to be.

—Chris Morante
Senior Pastor, Evangel Church, Scotch Plains, NJ

John Kotter, in his book *What Leaders Really Do*, wrote that "I am completely convinced that most organizations today lack the leadership they need." I wonder if some of that is true because those same organizations overlook female leaders like Marsha Mansour. Marsha has proven to be a beyond-her-years wise leader. She is a refreshingly candid female spiritual leader. Her accomplishments speak for themselves. The body of Christ needs more leaders like her. She and Deborah, the biblical judge, would make a great pair. I am deeply proud of her and thank God for her life and giftedness.

—Frank Reitzel Jr.
Executive Secretary, the New Jersey District Council of the Assemblies of God

THE
COURAGE
TO
LEAD

THE
COURAGE
TO
LEAD

Marsha M Mansour

REDEMPTION
PRESS

Published by Redemption Press, PO Box 427, Enumclaw, WA 98022

Toll Free (844) 2REDEEM (273-3336)

Redemption Press is honored to present this title in partnership with the author. The views expressed or implied in this work are those of the author. Redemption Press provides our imprint seal representing design excellence, creative content, and high quality production.

All Scripture quotations, unless otherwise indicated, are taken from the New King James Version®. Copyright © 1982 by Thomas Nelson. Used by permission. All rights reserved.

Scripture quotations marked NIV are taken from the Holy Bible, New International Version®, NIV® Copyright ©1973, 1978, 1984, 2011 by Biblica, Inc.® Used by permission. All rights reserved worldwide.

Note: The author has set specific words in the Scriptures in *italic* type for emphasis at his discretion.

ISBN: 978-1-68314-847-0 (Paperback)
978-1-68314-848-7 (ePub)
978-1-68314-849-4 (Mobi)

Library of Congress Catalog Card Number: 2019939520

Contents

Foreword

THERE ARE LEADERS, AND then there are dynamic leaders. Marsha Mansour is a dynamic leader.

Marsha doesn't just release others into life and leadership—she launches them! By inspiring others to live out their full potential, Marsha relentlessly speaks the truth in love. She demonstrates her authenticity, genuinely caring for people's hearts and spiritually mothering many.

Marsha's dynamic leadership has been forged in times of obscurity, submitting to challenging seasons. She obeys when it's not popular or easy. Life experiences have given Marsha the unique ability to speak from deep wells of wisdom paired with scriptural insights. She lives out the biblical principle of honor.

Marsha leaves an indelible mark on everyone with whom she comes in contact. I'm honored to know her as a person, pastor, and even more, as my friend.

—Pastor Stephanie Martinez,
President of Heart Exposed Music

Introduction

WHEN WE THINK OF leadership, what is the first thing that comes to our minds? Character qualities? An exceptional leadership quote? Maybe we think of the church or organization we are in charge of. When I think of leadership, I think of courage. Yes, courage. Great leadership requires great courage! Joshua 1:9 is by far one of my favorite Bible verses and one of the most quoted. It speaks right to a heart of a leader and gives the core value needed to lead and lead well: "Have I not commanded you? Be strong and courageous. Do not be terrified; do not be discouraged, for the Lord your God will be with you wherever you go."

I love the spirit of Joshua. I love the heart of Joshua. And so in Joshua chapter 1, God is instructing Joshua on how to lead the people of Israel. Moses has died, and He's preparing Joshua now to be his successor. He instructs how they will take the Promised Land. (Remember, Moses led them to the border, but he didn't lead them all the way in; Joshua was the one who brought Israel into the Promised Land.)

Moses did not have an easy job with Israel! They fought him every step. As a matter of fact, they had already reached the Promised Land forty years prior but did not have the courage to take it! Only Joshua and his buddy Caleb truly believed in and were willing to fight for the promises of God. It was for this reason they wandered for forty years. Moses had to lead a stubborn, rebellious, and fearful people until they either became the men and women God had called them to be, or they died off! What a leadership school for Joshua to learn from as he watched the good, the bad, and the ugly. He learned what to do from Moses and more importantly what not to do! Good leaders look for opportunities to learn from both the right things and the wrong. Not all mentoring happens by watching good leadership. Sometimes watching leaders' mistakes teaches us in greater ways.

Now Moses has died, and Joshua has to take all he has learned and apply it to lead five million people into the will of God. That's a pretty tall task.

As they were coming up to Joshua's first steps as their new leader, they ironically came back to the same spot where they failed before. However, this time God starts them off with the missing ingredient that cost them the Promised Land the first time: courage! The Lord starts off the chapter by saying, "Joshua be strong, and be of good courage. I'm going to give you every place where you put your foot. Don't move from the left to the right. Keep the law I've put in front of you. Walk strong. Meditate on it; you'll prosper. Just keep my word in your heart." And then He tells him again, "Be strong and of good courage. I'm going to be with you; I'm not going to leave you. I'll never forsake you."

God keeps giving Joshua more and more instructions, and in verse 9 we come to the verse I want to talk about. Joshua 1:9 says, "Have I not commanded you? Be strong. Be of good courage. Do not be dismayed, do not be afraid for the Lord your God will go with you wherever you go." It's interesting that the Lord says to Joshua three times, "Be strong, be of good courage." But the third time, He adds this sentence before it: "Have I not commanded you?" We don't talk about that verse a lot, but the Lord is actually giving him a command. He must be strong and of good courage. It wasn't an option. It wasn't a choice. If he was going to be the leader God called him to be, and if he was going to lead Israel through the things God had for them, strength and courage weren't an option. They were a command.

Today, any true, godly leader must possess courage. I have been in leadership for more years than I want to say, and I face situations, issues, and decisions weekly that require enormous amounts of courage to navigate. Leadership is not for the faint of heart, because it requires courage, and too often leaders take the easy way out. They would rather take a let's-see-what-will-happen approach. Friend, that is not leadership. Leadership makes bold, God-decisions with the trust and confidence that the Lord empowers them. They do the God thing no matter what and inspire those they are leading to do the same.

Leader, anything you want to accomplish for God, any place you want to lead people, if you want to be who Jesus has called you to be as a believer and as a leader, being strong and being courageous are not options. You must be strong and of good courage. He has commanded you to be these things, and the reason you can be strong and the reason you can have courage is the line right after: "Don't be afraid, don't be dismayed because the Lord God will go with you wherever you go."

Leader, remember that you never walk alone. You might feel alone, but that's a lie from the Enemy. You are never alone. The Lord Jesus walks with you every moment and every day. And so because He walks with you, you don't have to be afraid. You don't have to be dismayed. You can be strong. You can be courageous. Leadership can be lonely, but don't mistake the lonely times with being alone. Making courageous decisions will set you apart and give you some time by yourself, but the Lord is always with the man or woman of God as they lead for Him.

My heart in writing this book is to ignite and infuse the hearts of leaders with courage! It is time for strong, godly, Spirit-led leadership. I truly believe that courage is a position of the heart, and so you will find this book dealing with the heart and principles of leaders more than simply a how-to book. I want to walk us through principles that can govern our hearts and help us lead with confidence. I have watched too many leaders burn out or fail simply because they don't have governing principles to guard them. My prayer is to come alongside leaders and empower them for longevity and godly success!

As you prepare to read and study this book, I want to remind you that God Himself commands you to be strong and be courageous. So do that today, leader. Do it this week. Do it always! Remind yourself: Has He not commanded me to be strong and of good courage? Has He told me not to be afraid and not to be dismayed because He's going to be with me wherever I go? What land do you need to possess? What things do you need to walk around? What Jerichos do you need to walk around and take authority over? What do you need strength for this week? This year? Command yourself. You know, then you need to declare, "God has given me a mandate, and I'm going to take it. I'm going to be strong and of good courage. I'm not going to be afraid. I'm not going to be dismayed because the Lord God is going to go with me wherever I go. I never walk alone."

I want you to be the leader God has called you to be. Be strong and of good courage, child of God. Possess the land in front of you. Walk in victory. Walk in everything God has for you. Do not be afraid. Do not be dismayed, for the Lord goes with you everywhere you go. And most importantly, lead others around you to do the same!

His servant,

Rev. Marsha Mansour

CHAPTER ONE

Building the Kingdom System by System

BUILDING THE KINGDOM GOD has called us to as leaders is important because we don't just want to build quickly—we want to build well. So many times, though, when building something fresh, new, and exciting, we try to build too quickly, and that doesn't seem to work as well. That may suit cities and towns with booming subdivisions where homes are built quickly so people moving into the area can have a place to live. That may be fine for cities and towns to erect massive structures for the next greatest restaurant or department store to appeal to the masses. But it doesn't work as well for leaders in building their churches, because a church built for the Kingdom should be long lasting and produce great fruit. As leaders, like those who build cities and towns, we want to build our work quickly because we want fruit, we want people to fill our churches, we may want financial gain, or we simply want to be successful. But these desires are real errors, and they are not the reason to build the Kingdom. We build the Kingdom for God's glory only. And because of that, we need to build the Kingdom well and build it system by system. Often, the enemy to building well is building quickly.

Building the Kingdom System by System

Building the Kingdom system by system is like building a tower of blocks with all sorts of sizes. If we place the smallest blocks as the foundation, the tower will topple. But if we put the biggest and strongest block at the foundation and work our way up, then we will have a bulwark. The way to build well is system by system. Building well involves systems that are both sustainable and reproducible. *Sustainable* and *reproducible* are terms that leaders must understand well and model in their leadership. Let's break down these terms so we can understand together.

Sustainable: The dictionary definition of *sustainable* is anything that relates to a consistent method. A sustainable system moves easily and moves without you, the leader, needing to be present. A sustainable system involves a few factors. The first factor is that the system is not built around the leader or around a personality but is built so that it makes sense. Anyone can walk into the system and figure out how it works because it's clear and concise with steps to follow or instructions for troubleshooting. Any leader can step in and figure out how to make things work because the system doesn't require specific people to run things. That's a sustainable ministry, and that's what you want. The second factor is that a system should be able to run long-term; that's what *sustainable* means. If the ministry fizzles the year after I leave, that means I didn't make it sustainable. A sustainable system should have a long-term effect, and the ministry should be able to last for a long time; it shouldn't fizzle once a key person walks out of it. It should be easy to learn. A ministry should be so sustainable that it can also be reproduced by anyone else who comes after you.

Reproducible: Something is *reproducible* if it can be reproduced or copied. What does that mean for leaders? Anyone who works under you should be able to reproduce what you're doing; therefore, you must create a reproducible system. Your reproducible formula is a system that can be planted anywhere you go.

Putting the System into Practice

I get the privilege every year of running a Vacation Bible School at my church. We run Vacation Bible School for about eight hundred children and three hundred leaders. Both sustainable and reproducible systems exist within my VBS because it can operate without me. The system is clear, the methodology is clear, and the steps are obvious to those who are watching. No one has to struggle to figure out my system; it's sustainable. We have a system where the children move in modules every twenty minutes. What that means is crafts, recreation, and the lesson time all happen at the same time. For example, fourth grade will be in crafts, third grade will be in lesson time, and in twenty minutes, they switch. That allows me to have a high number of children and high excitement with lower chances of children getting bored. Also, the team is invested the whole time.

This type of system is also reproducible because I've taken our VBS system and used it all around the world: the same system, the same module schedule, the same way of building up leaders and coordinators and setting up responsibilities. It is reproducible. I have taken it to Africa, India, and Mexico, and we've used it in all our neighboring cities. We've done something called VBS Outside Our Borders where we take our Vacation Bible School, find a church that can't do Vacation Bible School the way we do, and we empower that church so that their system becomes reproducible. We get to watch those churches continue to build what we've taught them. It's reproducible, and it becomes easy because there is always something moving ahead.

The system is always able to be moved and reproduced. A key way to truly do that is to always have someone coming up underneath you. Someone should always be training underneath you. If everything lives and dies with you as a leader, you are now the cap for that ministry. You've created its own blockage. It won't grow past you. But if you're constantly reproducing yourself and constantly training, giving responsibility to, and releasing people into the ministry, then you're constantly reproducing the ministry, ensuring that the ministry won't have a cap. Without a cap, your ministry will grow strong, fertile, and with many, many branches. So it's key that as you're building, the ministry is a sustainable and reproducible system that includes training others under you even though this means that you are essentially building yourself out of a job.

Building Yourself out of a Job

If you are building your church or ministry properly, you are truly building yourself right out of a job. Now before you are alarmed, let me say that it's actually a good thing because that's what a sustainable, reproducible ministry does. It builds the leader out of the job because if he or she is constantly empowering, releasing, and giving responsibilities to others that cause the ministry to be reproduced, the system and the ministry will carry forward even though the leader becomes obsolete. That's really how you want to build a ministry.

I know for many leaders that's scary because you may be thinking, if I build myself out of a job, then what do I do? Well, when you build yourself out of your job, God gives you more ministry, and then it works like a wheel. As you release people to where God has called them, create sustainable and reproducible ministries, and build yourself out of a job, God can then give you more. God can put more ministry into your hands because you've proven trustworthy in building His house. Reproducible systems allow us to be better leaders and build with longevity. When we don't build with these ideals and we allow the needs of the ministry to dictate how we build, we run the risk of building what I call one-hit wonders.

Don't Live on One-Hit Wonders

As we have seen, systems are really, really important. Another incredibly important reason is that they help protect our teams from burnout and frustration. At the first sight of success in our ministry, we run into the risk of thinking we're exclusive to building our ministry. Ministries that have high turnover rates usually operate with poor systems and with a leader who thinks they are exclusive to its success. Poor systems put us in the one-hit wonder world. What is a one-hit wonder? One-hit wonders are event-driven ministries. If an event is coming up, the leader thinks they have to make the event work. They get the job done but without counting the cost. It is run at a hundred miles an hour, get it done, and figure out the issues later. That's called a one-hit wonder.

Don't think because you got the job done for one event that you actually have a system that works. That only means you're good at putting things together at the last minute. Rather, ministry we do for the Lord should be excellent and shouldn't be a series of one-hit wonders. It shouldn't be something that I throw together and make happen, and because it looks good, think I have a working system.

You never want to operate on a system that is pieced together. You always want to operate from a system that exists and works well, so that each time an event comes up, it doesn't overwhelm you or your team. You have systems in place so that each time an event comes up, it just falls into the filter of the system, and it works. But if you have to recreate the system each single time, something is wrong with your system. If you have poor systems, you will never gain quality leaders or have longevity in what you are building.

Here are some questions to ask yourself to ensure your system works or to gauge how to do it differently: Was what I did excellent? Was it done in a timely manner? Was it done with the right preparation? Could someone else do it if I was away? Answering those questions will tell you if the system you have in place works so all can understand it.

Understand How Systems Work

It is important to understand that systems are driven by principles. Because it is impossible to give a system for every single scenario, you have to build your system around over-arching principles. For example, if you're a leader of the children's ministry, one of your key overarching principles is safety. Now your systems are built around safety. Another key principle in your system can be structure. If you're running assimilation, what is your key principle? Your key principle is that people feel connected. These kinds of principles now govern the systems you build. Those are systems that work because once your team understands the root of the principle, the system now makes sense. Conversely, if a system is arbitrary, it's up in the air and doesn't have a root or principle behind it, then the system becomes flexible and movable because people don't understand the root of it. But if you create a system that's built around safety, as I do for our children's ministry, then the team understands everything that operates out of it. They inadvertently say, "Oh, she's doing this because of safety," and it's no longer my own principle because it now becomes the team's principle. Root principles are crucial when you're building systems. Why? So people can understand your system and the vision behind why you do what you do.

Vision behind Building a Proper System

When you build proper systems that are principle-rooted, it gives you a platform of vision that allows workers (future leaders) to come alongside you and help build what God has called you to build. We have watched God reproduce the

Vacation Bible School I spoke of all over New Jersey and New York. From that one VBS, we are able to feed ten to twelve other Vacation Bible Schools just in our area, not counting the four or five Vacation Bible Schools we do each year around the world. We've done them in Guatemala. We've done them all over the place. Why? Because we have a system in place where people have bought into the vision of VBS. The principle purpose of VBS is letting children fall in love with Jesus. I don't have workers—I have leaders who help facilitate that experience for the children and then from there, we see great and mighty things.

As a leader, if you sell work, labor, or a need, you only end up with workers. People will come because you have a need. But if you sell vision you'll end up with leaders because vision drives any ministry. Therefore, if people understand the vision behind your systems, why you do them the way you do, then you're going to end up with leaders who not only do what you do but build on what you do and make it better. If you sell work or labor, yes, they'll come, and they'll serve because people are good, and they want to serve, but you'll never end up with leaders. But if you saying things like, "We want to build a church where our children can fall in love with Jesus, learn the Word of God, and grow in the things of the Spirit. I need people who are going to help me create a place where God can meet these children with His love and change their lives forever," you will end up with leaders, not workers, because leaders respond to vision. Leaders must have vision to build systems.

In one of the children's ministries I had the honor of building, the church had wonderful children's workers but no real leaders. I quickly learned why. They would recruit by saying things like, "Come help us with the children's ministry; we need help." So they got beautiful workers but no leaders. I had to flip all that on its ear. We started recruiting by saying things like, "Do you want to be part of leading this generation to Jesus? Do you want to be part of a team that gets to pour life into amazing children?" Quickly, we started seeing leaders sign up left and right. We were speaking their language, and they were responding. Within a few short years we had tons of leaders and could build on their backs ever more ministry. Always drive with vision.

Problems When Building a System

When you're building systems, there are some potential problems to look out for. Sometimes you may build too many layers around a certain system. When you make something super layered, the system doesn't make a whole lot of sense. Be careful about how many layers you have. You want to layer the system just enough so that it is safe, and it makes sense. Three key questions to ask yourself are: Is it sustainable? Is it reproducible? Can people understand it?

Let's discuss a few potential problems with too many layers and how to fix them. If it takes fifteen steps to baptize someone, it's layered too much. If it takes twenty-two steps to work in the children's ministry, something is wrong. If it takes five steps to work in the youth ministry, that's just about right. Each system should have clear, easy steps to follow. Each system should be layered just enough so that people can succeed in what they're called. Anything more than what is absolutely necessary for the particular system you're trying to put in place, and you've layered it too much. People have very busy lives, we have to make sure we can stick to our principles but also create great systems so that people can step into ministry and do it with all their hearts. We also have to create systems that are simple enough to understand but complicated enough to care for the ministries we've been trusted with. It's a dance, I know, but learning to layer just enough is something that'll make your ministry greatly succeed.

Keys for Building a Successful Ministry

To build a sustainable, reproducible ministry, a few keys are needed. But two are essential, and we must remember them in order to build a successful ministry. First, we must remember that we are building people. Sometimes pastors and leaders look at people as merely tools to make things work, or make the ministry a success, and that's a huge mistake. The people under you are to be valued and cared for by you as their leader. Many leaders are singularly minded at getting a task done, and they forget that people matter much more than the task. I have often seen leaders burn out those who work for them. The task is never more important than the people. We must always have a pulse on those who work for us and do our best to care for them. When they feel loved and cared for, everything works better.

Second, there's a key statement I believe is necessary for all leaders to live by. I actually got this quote from the movie, *Patriot*. In one of the scenes, the lead character is teaching his sons how to shoot a gun. He says, "How has Daddy taught you to shoot a gun?" The boys look at their dad and say, "Aim small, miss small." For me, as a leader, that's the way I build people. Our goal is to bring people under us who show potential and give them little opportunities to build ministry. Aim small so that if they miss, they miss small—if you give them a target too big to handle, you've set them up for failure. Aim small, miss small, and as they prove faithful and that they really do have ability and talent, then you can assess what they have and what they don't have. From there, you can build them and build them and build them.

Let these be two key principles in your leadership: build people, and aim small, miss small. With that in mind, let's look at some keys for building a successful ministry.

Key 1—People Need True Pastors and Leaders

It doesn't matter what gift or what talent people in your ministry bring to the table, they need a pastor and a leader. Without an effective pastor and leader, ministries and churches fizzle out and do not extend a measurable level of lasting success. What are some key roles for you as a pastor/leader? One role is to love on the people whom God's entrusted to you. The people within your ministry have been entrusted into your care by the Lord, so love them, and don't use them. Love them, and even when they can't give you anything, love them still. Another role is to take care of them. They're not there to take care of you. You are their leader, so take care of them. I have to tell you that as a leader, oftentimes when I've seen someone who serves under me go through a really hard time in their personal life, I've actually fired them from ministry. I've said, "You are a fantastic leader, but your personal life has exploded, and I want to give you room now to grow. I want to give you room to deal with what's going on in your life." I've let them go, and I have to tell you that each time I've done that, they've cried, and it wasn't out of sadness, it was out of, "Wow, I can't believe you love me so much that you'd lose me from the ministry in order to take care of me." The loyalty that is purchased then is priceless.

As you love and care for the people under you, they will see your loyalty because you have chosen to walk with them, work with them, and make them a priority. And because you love and care for them, they will want to help pour into the ministries and tasks you're building and carry it onto the next generation. Thus, any system will only work if you truly build people. Reproduce people, put people under you that have giftings and talents, but invest in them regardless of what they can do for you, and you will be an excellent builder and a truly effective leader.

Key 2—Build a Common Language

Each culture starts with speaking the same language, and building ministry with its own common language is no different. There should be a language among your people that sounds like you. If you were to come to the churches that I've served in, you will hear my verbiage come out of those leaders. Why? Because I've built common language around it. I was saved when I was four years old, and something I always say is that the generation of children and youth in any church are not the generation of tomorrow, they're the generation of today. If you come to any church I've served in, you would hear that. We're not looking to build the generation of tomorrow; we're building the generation of today. That's part of my common language.

When you're building your ministry and building up people, create a common language among your ministries. A language that is clear will become part of the ministry culture. Language will help build a reproducible ministry because people then will always lean into the language; it becomes part of the DNA and helps to form behavior which also helps to create core values that build forward.

Key 3—Build Core Values

When building your system, it's important to build core values. Build the values and the principles that matter to you as a leader, and that will further your ministry's cause.

For me and my ministry, a key value is loyalty. The leaders training under me know that I'm loyal to them to a fault, which gives them confidence when they serve. And in developing the key value of loyalty, the leaders training under me exude confidence when they talk because they understand that I have their backs. In turn, they build loyalty toward me. I don't have to tell them to be loyal; I simply demonstrate it, and because that's one of my key values, it comes back to me.

Another key value in my ministry is excellence. I'm not a perfectionist, and I'm not all in the details, but I want things done well. Because striving for excellence is also part of my personal values, it shows up in my ministry, and it creates a reproducible ministry. I'll hear my leaders say things like, "It doesn't have to be perfect. You just have to do your best." And doing our best means that things will always move forward. Every ministry has key values. It is important for you to identify them and foster them. It will build continuity, strength, confidence, and durability. However, make sure they are true values, things that can actually be seen, not a wish list. That doesn't mean you do this 100 percent of the time but pretty close.

Key 4—Build Forward

Another key when building a system is to build forward. Don't build backward—build forward. It doesn't matter how successful your ministry is—it will die if you don't build forward. God is always moving us forward, so always in your heart and your head, move your ministry and people forward. What's the next step? Where's the next place? God, what more do you have for this ministry? How can I expand? Ask God how you can build forward because you believe He has more. Build systems that are not always complete in themselves. What do I mean by that? Leave room for things to move forward, for things to accelerate, and for things to come out of the box. Don't seal things; always leave room for growth. Never act like the ministry is complete; always be willing to develop and build out. Give room for out-of-the-box thinking and forward motion.

Finally, a surefire way to know you are building your ministry forward is to always make sure to build a reproducible system. Build places for the younger generation to help lead right in the midst of your ministry. At my Vacation Bible School, we have a woman who leads worship, but right beside her is one of my young adults helping lead worship. Right beside the young adult is one of my youth leading worship, and right beside the youth is one of our children. Four stages of life are represented on the platform every time we do Vacation Bible School. Why? Because I'm building into the next generation to ensure that particular system is automatically reproducible. When the woman who was leading was no longer able, the young adult was ready to step right into her position and lead without missing a beat because we had built a reproducible ministry.

Each of my leaders serving under me has someone serving under them, ready to reproduce and build the ministry. The second person's job, then, is to find the third person, and so on. In doing so, everyone in the ministry is constantly building and reproducing a strong, powerful ministry that's moving forward for the Kingdom. And these people bring freshness, zeal, and new ideas that help everything to move forward. Never talk about the past more than the future.

Conclusion

I want to encourage you as we end this chapter that it is all about building the Kingdom well. We don't want to just build fast. We want to build it strong because the Kingdom has everything to do with souls and with lives; therefore, we want to build the ministry system by system, person by person. Leader, you must determine in your heart that you want to build sustainable, reproducible ministries that allow ministries to be places of transformation.

Well-built systems create safety within your ministry or organization. The church should be a safe place—when systems are solid and procedures are clear in how the ministry works and operates, there's an umbrella of safety, and transformation can happen.

Transformation happens in safe places. People do not become vulnerable or transparent in unsafe places because they don't want to get hurt. But when they walk into a church or a meeting or where Christian activity is happening and it feels safe, it creates an environment for vulnerability, and within that vulnerability, transformation happens. Everything we do as leaders should create places where transformation happens. So if you love and care for people and you build strong systems that are sustainable and reproducible, you will automatically create safety. As you create safety, you will see transformation come out of your ministry like you've never seen it before. Leader and child of God, build your ministry and people well.

CHAPTER TWO

Honor and Authority

ECONOMIES WORK DIFFERENTLY ACROSS various parts of the world. In the natural world, there is a way to earn money: you work, and you get a paycheck, hopefully. No one's ever satisfied with their paycheck, but that's the economy: I work. I get paid. I put money in the bank, and I write a check. No money in the bank: I write a check, and then I wear a nice orange suit. This is how the economy works on planet Earth. When I travel to Guadalajara on mission trips, there is an economy that works there. Pesos and different types of dollars, but at the end of the day, there is an exchange system that's understood. When I go to parts of Africa, some regions do not use money. They literally use chickens, but that's their economy. That's how exchange happens there. The same is true for leaders; there is an economy in Heaven that grows your leadership. It advances you and causes you to grow in leaps and bounds!

Heaven's Economy

There is an economy that works in Heaven where the Kingdom of God and the people of God grow personally and in leadership. Heaven's economy does not happen by money, position, or from things that work in the world. There is an economy for Heaven in relation to a Kingdom philosophy that is completely different from anything else in terms of earthly wisdom. For example, in the economy of Earth, you look out for number one. You look for someone to advance you, and you look for opportunities to help push your way through. Conversely, in the Kingdom of Heaven, the economy is that I prefer my brother over myself. On Earth it's an eye for an eye, a tooth for a tooth, but in the economy of Heaven, you slap me on this cheek, I give you the other one. In the economy of Earth, you do me wrong, I do you wrong as well. In Heaven, I do not repay evil for evil, but overcome evil with good. Those are some of the differences between the Kingdom economy and Earth's economy.

Principles of Advancement and Leadership

Now let's explore the economy of Heaven as it applies to advancement and leadership. A huge part of the leadership economy falls under honor and authority. Together, these words must be clearly understood by anyone who feels God has a pull on them for the mantle of leadership. Leadership will not advance any other way. They don't advance by your giftings. If you have not learned the principles of honor and authority, your giftings will take you to a place where you will crash and burn. I've watched it a million times. I have friends who failed in ministry because they didn't understand this. I know of situations right now where leaders are literally on their way out of the ministry because they don't understand this principle, or they won't yield to it. True, godly leadership must understand this principle and yield to it.

God's Kingdom is not advanced by my gifts, my talents, my abilities, or my smarts. It's advanced by God's economy. His economy is an economy of honor and authority. If we can understand these two synonymous principles, we can move forward in leading our churches, people, and ministries.

Understanding Honor

Let's look at honor for a bit. Honor is a huge part of what I experience because I've never been a senior pastor. I have always been a subordinate pastor. I am a female. I am Egyptian. I am currently single. Should I give you any more accolades after my name? There is always this position of being subordinate, being a female, being ethnic, and being single. I have always worked in that role. I have been in authority, but under someone else since I was nineteen. Throughout my entire ministry career, I have always served under a senior pastor.

I've worked under eight pastors. Of the eight, three were men of God, on fire, loved Jesus, and had right character. I'll leave the others for God to judge, but I was working under them. I was their subordinate, and I had to honor them. See, I understood the economy of leadership, and I chose to walk in it. One particular example where I had to show great honor happened when I worked as a youth pastor at an ethnic church. I had been there for about two years, and we had just started doing outreaches into the community. On one particular Sunday outreach, my youth kids were so excited because they led three teenagers to the Lord. They brought them back to church with them and everyone was cheering and welcoming them. It was a great atmosphere.

After a few moments, the senior pastor sent for me. My initial thought was that he was going to be excited with everyone else and wanted to ask me privately what had happened. I was wrong. Instantly he started in with questions like, "What are you doing? How could you allow this to happen?"

I had no idea what he was talking about.

He was furious. Finally, he asked the nationality of those three kids, and I innocently answered that they were Hispanic.

He said, "Don't you know the name on this church? It's not a Hispanic church. Send them back to their church and their people!" I couldn't believe my ears. As if it couldn't get any worse, he told me they were not welcome here and to throw them out.

I was in my early twenties when this happened, and nothing in Bible school had prepared me for this moment. What in the world do I do? I was in shock, and I was angry and disappointed.

The senior pastor stood right in my face, demanding that I throw them out. All I knew to do in that moment was to lean on the Lord, so I began to pray frantically in my head. Then I felt the calm of the Holy Spirit, and I just heard a very quick sentence. I turned to the pastor and calmly said, "Pastor I can't throw them out. This isn't my house; it's your house, and if you don't want someone in your house, *you're* going to have to throw them out."

He just stared at me and asked me to repeat what I just said.

I simply said the same thing again.

He was angry with me, but he couldn't speak. My answer had silenced him. Actually, the Holy Spirit's answer silenced him.

We walked out of that office where he sheepishly went up to the three teenagers, greeted them, and welcome them to the church. They stayed as part of our church family for years. They never knew of that incident nor did anyone else.

The Holy Spirit had empowered me in that moment. I did not dishonor the pastor, but I was also able to guard the youth. You may ask yourself why I would work there with such a leader. God placed me there! He called me there. You know what my role was? To honor the leadership over me even if they were not worthy of honor in my opinion. I was not there to expose them or call them out. I was there to honor them and let the Holy Spirit handle the rest. Leader, He will empower you too, the same way He empowered Jesus.

Biblical Example of Honor

In the story of David and Saul, David was anointed by Samuel the prophet to be the future king of Israel. That meant in the Heavens, David was the king of Israel, but on Earth, Saul was the current king. Saul found out about David being anointed king and tried to kill him twenty-two times but failed each time. Then one day, Saul was killed, and the report came to David. What did he do? Saul had hunted and tried to kill him for years; what would David now do with this information? David killed the man who killed Saul! You'd think David would have thrown a party because Saul had hunted David, attacked him, and threw spears at him. You'd think David would be relieved. But David says to the man who killed Saul, "You touched God's anointed." 1 Samuel 24:6 is the first time we see this verbiage. What does this mean? It's honor—David understood the economy of leadership, and because David honored Saul, God blessed David's steps. David understood how the Kingdom should be advanced, and even when he had every opportunity to take the Kingdom, he didn't.

There was a day that Saul was in his most vulnerable state. David was hiding in a cave, and Saul came into the cave to relieve himself. That means he was going to the bathroom. Talk about the most vulnerable position you could possibly be in. David was close enough to touch the edge of Saul's garment. The Bible says that he actually cut off a piece of the garment, and the second he did so his heart broke because it was wrong. David says out loud to Saul, "King, look how close I got to you, but I will never touch you again. Long live King Saul."

You know what David's friends told him? "You're crazy. You're crazy. God has given you the Kingdom in your hands. Look how easy it would have been to kill your enemy, and you didn't do it" (1 Samuel 24:3, author's paraphrase)." But David understood that revenge was the world's economy. David chose Heaven's economy to honor the man God had chosen to be king and to honor him until God removed him.

As a leader in ministry, God will hand you everything in time, but you simply must do what's right. I have never sought a position in ministry, and yet God has tapped me on the shoulder each time, and God has blessed me every single time. I looked for ways to learn how God's economy operated in Heaven and then live it out. Here David operated in the same economy of God, and the kingdom of Israel was handed to him. King David knew God would reward him for doing the God thing. Leader, it is always a question of honor.

Personal Example of Honor

In one of the churches I worked in, the pastor wasn't a man of God. He had allowed pride to enter his heart, and he had become arrogant and puffed up. In this church, the youth and children were not important. I was the youth and children's pastor. So, imagine the surprise when God sent revival in the midst of all this. I was at the church seven months and revival happened. Thirty-five kids were baptized in the Holy Spirit in one service. My kids wanted to drop out of school because they were ready to go preach to the ends of the earth. They were on fire for God.

At the time, I had two secular jobs because the church couldn't pay me a salary. Here I was, working in a church where the pastor didn't care about any of the children. The families were upset because they didn't see money going into the children's program, so at our church business meeting, they begin to ask questions. I was in the back of the church, and the pastor pulled up a business report which stated that the church had paid $34,000 to the youth and children's ministry. That was a lie as far as I knew.

The families did not believe the pastor.

I was in the back, trying to run out the door because I was in charge of the ministries they'd spoken about.

Finally, the pastor got defensive and yelled to me "Pastor Marsha, didn't I spend $34,000 on the youth and children's ministry this year?"

How many of you at that point would want the floor to open and swallow you up? I stood there, wanting just that, but I prayed, "Lord, you have to help me because if I say yes, that's a blatant lie. If I say no, I've split the church because the church will know that he's lying." I prayed, "Lord, give me wisdom." I looked at him and said, "You know what, I really have no idea what was spent by this church on the youth and children. I know what I spent, but I have no idea about any other money."

I answered with honor and respect.

The pastor didn't think so. He thought I should have lied. That was a conversation for later, but in that moment, I had a decision to make. Either I'm going to split the body of Christ, or I'm going to let God judge him. I let God judge him. That pastor lost it all. He lost the church. He lost the building. He lost the people, but it wasn't because of my answer. If you have a chance to protect the church body, protect the church body. Even at your own cost, protect the body. Protect the bride of Christ.

In that moment during the church business meeting, I had to decide if I would split the church for my own gain or ask the Lord to help me honor the church and protect it, letting the Lord deal with the fallout should it happen. I chose to ask for the Lord's help, and He protected me. It wasn't long after that everything fell to the ground. But I'm not responsible for what anyone over me does. I'm responsible for what I do. We must always carry the weight of our words and actions. We must act with honor and respect, protecting the church body at all times.

Honor Conclusion

Honoring the authorities who are placed in front of us is a system that we've forgotten in the church. We operate by questioning authority and challenging them, and if we don't agree, we badmouth them. God wants us to treat people with honor. I treat those in the church who are of senior age with honor. Not only do I show those in authority and seniors honor, but I also show honor to those members who have lived the faith for a while, as well as those who have walked with God a long time. If you have walked with God for forty years, you have something to share with me. You have something to teach me.

There is a system of honor that we in the church have forgotten. We want everything fast and quick and high tech. For instance, so what if Grandpa can't turn on YouTube, he can teach you how to pray. So what if Grandma doesn't know how to operate a smart TV, she can teach you what it is to be a woman of God. The mamas and daddies of the church need to be treated with honor as well. Scripture even set up the model that the older should be teaching the younger. The mothers should be teaching the daughters. The Naomis teaching the Ruths. It should be the Pauls teaching the Timothys. Such is a system of honor where we must put aside our self-focused attitude, and we as leaders of the church need to bring back the level of honor so that everyone involved in the church can walk in the economy of God.

Understanding Honor and Authority Together

If we need to incorporate the system of honor back into the church, then we need to understand the system of authority. Whether you are a pastor, deacon, Sunday school teacher, or have any sort of ministry in the church or even in the business world, you have leadership; therefore, you have authority. And with authority comes great judgment. The Bible is clear that those in authority will be judged greater than others. If anyone in leadership leads poorly, then let God take care of them. Let God deal with it appropriately. Don't worry, because your responsibility is the condition of your heart. If we understand the economy of God, whatever we do is our business. I am responsible for my business. You see, with authority comes great responsibility, so let God weigh out these things.

Remember the church I was telling you about where they had falsified spending $34,000 on the children's ministry? One day, my dear friend Pastor Walter called me to go work with him at a different church. We walked through a series of interviews together, and I finally gave my resignation at the church where I currently worked as the children's pastor. Surprisingly, no one on the board or among the deacons and the pastoral staff wished me well with my new ministry. Instead, they simply gave me two weeks to leave. I offered to stay three months, but they basically told me to get out. For two weeks leading up to my departure, I said nothing. I walked in the way I had walked the whole time I was there. I didn't change even though those in authority over me had altered their attitudes. That's their responsibility. It was my choice to walk in honor and to honor their authority until the day I walked out of that building because my life is about pleasing God and walking in His economy.

On my last Sunday, no one said goodbye to me except for the kids, the youth, and their parents. Everyone else walked out the door. It was my practice after each Sunday service to clean the church, turn off the heat, and check the water and stove top. There was a certain system I had because it was a small church. After my final youth service, I did everything normally: the kids and I cleaned up together, I walked outside, and I put the church keys in the mailbox. We extended our hands and prayed over the church. I blessed it, and I left. You know why? Because I understand the economy of God. I didn't walk out on my last day saying, "Forget them. If this is how they treated me, they can clean their own church. Here are their keys. I'm out." No. I must understand the economy of God and live in that economy because I am responsible for my own reaction.

Luke, chapter 5, talks about the story of Jesus and the multitude. The crowd had pressed against Jesus so much as He was teaching that He had to get into one of the empty boats docked at the lake and continue teaching from there. That empty boat belonged to Simon (later to be named Peter). When Jesus finished speaking, He said to Simon, "Launch out into the deep and let down your nets for a catch" (Luke 5:4). Simon told

Jesus they had tried catching fish all night and hadn't caught anything, but he knew Jesus's reputation, so he launched his net anyway. Soon, though, he had to have the other fishermen help him pull in the nets because of how many fish they had caught. What had been empty boats began to sink from all the fish!

After Simon saw what Jesus had done, he fell down at Jesus's feet and said, "Depart from me, for I am a sinful man, O Lord" (Luke 5:8). Clearly, he was amazed at the number of fishes they had caught and recognized that Jesus made that happen for them.

This is not normally a story in which you talk about honor; however, let's examine it. At first, Simon did not know who Jesus truly was. When Jesus told Simon to lower the nets on the other side of the boat, Simon, who was a master fisherman, said they had already been out fishing all night and had caught nothing. He knew more about fishing than anyone else around. Yet Simon shows Jesus honor by saying, "Nevertheless at Your word, I will let down the net" (Luke 5:5). He knew of Jesus and honored Him. He obeyed Jesus: he dropped his net and hauled in the biggest catch of his life. He had to get another boat to help him. Both boats began to sink under the burden of the huge catch. Why? Because Simon honored the Man of God. (He did not yet know that he was the Son of God.) God then chose to honor Simon. Likewise, when we choose to honor men and women of God, the authority He has placed over and around us, God then turns around and honors us.

Striving to Be the Most Influential Leader You Can Be

Now that we have covered the principles of honor and authority, we must explore the positions of leadership. John Maxwell, in his book *Developing the Leader within You*, describes these positions as the five levels of leadership.[1] Each level has a measure of influence; as the level raises, so does the influence. Each leader starts at level 1, however no leader should stay there. Each leader should strive to increase in their leadership and influence.

Leadership level 1 is called *positional*—we honor people simply because they have the position; they have a title. In the story above, that's what Simon did. He didn't know Jesus from a hole in the wall. He just knew that Jesus was a good teacher and a prophet, and He's done some miracles. He's special; Simon honors Him. But as he walks with Jesus, that changed. Jesus was a level 1 leader who became a level 5. What is level 5? This is the utmost leader you could ever be or ever honor. There are times in your life, you're going to have a level 1 leader, a level 2 leader, or a level 3 leader over you. You're going to have to honor them. It doesn't matter what level they are; what matters is the condition of your heart. What matters is that you are honoring God and acting appropriately.

I worked in a very difficult church for eight years. I worked with leaders who were difficult to work with. But I wouldn't exchange one minute of those experiences because they taught me the economy of Heaven. God will put us in places that

---

1. John Maxwell, *Developing the Leader within You*, special ed. (New York: HarperCollins Leadership, 2018).

demand us to honor those difficult leaders because He wants to teach us the economy of Heaven. Leadership advancement comes only through honor. It does not come by force. It does not come by other ways. It comes by honoring and walking and praying. Anything we want to do for the Kingdom comes by honor, no matter how honorable the person. Now as a leader, I should never be satisfied with being at level 1; that is basic leadership and produces very little fruit.

Let me give you another example of honor at different levels. I have had the privilege of speaking at women's conferences all around. Some were familiar places and some were new. On the first day at one unfamiliar church, I grabbed the female pastor and the woman in charge of the conference. I said, "I have looked all over your website to try and understand what you believe about the Spirit of God, but it's not there. So I need some parameters because I don't want to be disrespectful. I don't want to overstep what you believe."

With an astonished face, one of them said, "You're the guest?"

I said, "I'm a guest in your house. It's not my house. I don't walk into peoples' houses, open up their refrigerators, kick off my shoes, and act like it's all mine. I walk into someone's house with respect, and this is your house. So, what are my parameters?"

They were shocked, and the other said, "We know what you bring, we've researched you, and we know exactly who you are. Do whatever you want."

I said, "Are you sure? You're sure I can do whatever I want?"

They both responded, "Absolutely. We're honored for you to come."

In every church in which I speak, I don't want to assume I can do whatever I want because in God's Kingdom, I must honor the authority over me. Even in churches in which I am familiar with their faith and practice, I will still show honor and make sure what I plan to do is okay with them.

When our language becomes as such with one another, the Kingdom advances in you, and it advances around you because showing honor creates a safety net where God is able to move and allow things to change. When we are forceful and determined to press our way through, God doesn't honor that. When I'm honoring and respecting other leaders, I'm honoring the Lord. And though our situation may be good, bad, or indifferent, God placed us there, and we must learn how to show honor.

A Culture of Honor and Respect

As you begin to move with the things of God, learn this culture of honor and respect from a giving place. It's not an old-fashioned way of thinking as it's been represented for many years. Submission is how the Kingdom advances. Honor is how the Kingdom advances. It has never been advanced by force. It has never been advanced by talent. The Holy Spirit is a gentleman. We've painted Him out to be something very different, but He's a gentleman. He does not break down doors; He simply knocks. He will never force His will on you. He gives you a free will to choose because He's a gentleman. If the Holy Spirit operates from a level of honor, how much more should we as leaders operate from a level of honor, submission, and respect?

When I go on mission trips all over the world, I get to work in different places and see how honor is done in different countries. People in other countries know how to honor. They understand submission and authority.

One of the greatest miracles that ever happened in my life started with a choice I made to honor those over me! I was on a mission trip to Africa. We were doing a kid's crusade in an area that was 99 percent Muslim. The pastors in the area told me not to get my hopes up of having a lot of kids because of this. Rather than be disappointed, I knew that however many kids God brought would be enough for our crusade.

In Africa they don't advertise with posters. They advertise with loudspeakers as they drive down the road. The taxi driver yelled over the loudspeakers, announcing that there would be a children's crusade. But as we drove through the village, hundreds of kids were running beside the car, shouting, "Americans! Americans!" I was really surprised because there were many, many more than the pastors had said would be there. Literally, hundreds of kids all followed us to the crusade site.

At the meeting area, I gathered my eight helpers and told them to make circles of ten. But the kids just kept coming in. We eventually had to make circles of fifty and sixty kids. By the time we finished counting, we had a thousand children— a thousand Muslim children! Muslim women lined the back with the men along the side.

Now, the pastors began to panic. They told me our permit expired at six o'clock that night, and if we weren't out by 5:45, there would possibly be a riot, and the police wouldn't help us.

I assured them I would be done by 5:45.

Before I started the program, the pastors took me aside and one of them said, "We would appreciate it if you didn't say that Jesus is the Messiah. You can use any other word you want. You can use teacher, prophet, or king, but when you say Jesus is the Messiah, it is very clear to Muslim people that you are saying Jesus is the Son of God, and we don't know what their reaction would be."

I was quiet for a minute, and then I said, "What if the Lord tells me to say it? What do you want me to do?"

They responded: "Pastor, if the Holy Spirit tells you to say that, then say it. But please make sure it's the Holy Spirit who told you to say it."

I replied, "Okay. So I have your permission if the Holy Spirit tells me to say Jesus is the Messiah, I can?"

"Yes."

So we started the rally with music, dancing, stories, and snacks. In Africa, things like this don't last an hour or two. In Africa events last six hours or more. When we came to the story of salvation, I heard the voice of the Lord clear as day say, "Tell them I'm the Messiah."

I obeyed and said, "Jesus is the Messiah." The translator looked over at me then nodded his head and repeated after me. When he translated, of course, the pastors behind me understood.

I felt their breath leave them.

You know what happened? Nothing! You could hear a pin drop!

The Lord said, "Say it again."

So I said, "Jesus is the Messiah."

The translator smiled, a big smirk on his face, as he translated what I said.

Then I asked, "How many of you want to know Jesus the Messiah as your own Messiah?"

Every hand went up! One thousand children raised their hands, accepting the Lord. The moms on the side took their head coverings off and lifted their hands to accept the Lord. The fathers in the back just stood there.

Then I said, "Bow your heads," and they bowed their heads. All of them prayed to accept Jesus the Messiah.

You might be thinking, What does this story have to do with honor? I showed honor to them by getting their permission and their blessing to share that Jesus was the Messiah. I could have said, "How dare they restrict me from saying what I want to say. I came all this way." But it doesn't work that way. That's not how to advance the Kingdom. I was a guest and needed to honor the authority over me.

So at 5:45 p.m., we finished. I was done. Kids were blessed. God moved. Many children were healed right on the spot. People with asthma, which you see everywhere because of the dust, were healed. All around us, people were healed.

Right as we ended they put me in a car and said, "You gotta get out of here now." The permit was almost expired, and they feared for my safety.

We were driving down the road, and our driver was Muslim. There was a translator in the front seat, and I had a woman from my team with me. Then I heard the Holy Spirit say to me, "Pray for protection right now." So, I began to pray.

Unbeknownst to me, the Lord told the pastors back at the rally, "Pray for her."

In Africa, when criminals want to ambush your car, they block the road with small rocks stacked as high and deep as the car. The night was pitch black, and you couldn't see anything, including where the road started and ended.

As we were driving, I extended my hands to pray in the Spirit because I sensed something was off. Everyone in the car were also praying because now there was a spirit of unity in our hearts. We came up to a road that was completely blocked, but then we noticed men on both sides with torches. The driver's hands began to shake because he knew we are about to be attacked.

The Lord said to me, "Tell him to keep driving, not to slow down or speed up, just keep going. Keep going."

I tell the translator what the Lord had said to me, and he asked, "What?"

I said, "Keep going! Don't stop! Don't slow down! Keep going!"

The driver looked at me but did not stop. He kept going and didn't slow down. As he came up to the rocks, they split right down the middle and fell to either side! We drove straight through; the rocks parted like the Red Sea! Nothing touched us!

We drove farther, and the road was blocked again! We have truly been targeted. I turned to the driver: "Keep going! Don't stop! Don't slow down!"

He did it again. The rocks split right down the middle again, we drove right through, and were in awe. The road was blocked a third time, the driver does not even look at me. He just keeps going straight through and the rocks fell to both sides for the third time!

We pulled up to the hotel with not a scratch on us. We were completely safe. The driver turned to me and the translator and said, "Who do you serve?" We told him, and he gave his life to Jesus right there on the streets of Africa!

When the economy of God is working properly, the supernatural shows up. But when our flesh and arrogance, stubbornness and selfishness overtake us, things get messed up. Instead of clean water, it's muddy water. But when the economy of God is working properly and there is honor and respect for authority, then things advance the way they should. So as the child of God and leader you are today, understand what it is to live a lifestyle of honor.

The Culture of Authority

Now, let's flip the switch for a minute and talk about authority. Authority is a powerful tool because if you are in a place of authority in some shape, fashion, or form, you've been given influence along with that authority. And you must use that influence wisely. You've been given a gift; don't ever abuse the people under you.

As I shared at a women's conference one time: "Women have this beautiful fragrance that God gives them. They have the ability to speak life. Do you know that in one sentence, you can flip everything? With one sentence or one comment, you've now taken your influence and made it manipulative. When you've been given authority, you have the ability to bless or curse. It's one sentence that you'll speak into someone's spirit that'll stay for years because you have authority when that person respects you."

Even if it's level 1 leadership, they look at you with authority. You might have a leader you don't think too highly of, but they still have that positional place. Remember the elementary or high school teacher you didn't like? If that teacher had told you, "You're so dumb," you would remember that comment forever. As a leader, your interaction with those under you is important.

As a leader, we must learn to walk with grace and mercy. There will always be someone who ticks us off, but we can't react. If you have to, take a walk around the block to catch your breath. But understand that you are never meant to use your authority to manipulate or get back at people. Do not use your influence to make them dependent on you, your gifting, your talent, and your ability. Your authority and influence is meant to point them to Christ, to the cross, and to the Word of God. We must simply respond with honor and respect. Also, don't use your authority to advance yourself.

The perfect example of this is found in the story of Esther. King Ahasuerus was deciding between which of seven women, including Esther, he wanted to make his wife. The king's eunuch, who is nameless, prepared Esther to meet the king by showing her all the things the king liked: favorite fragrance, makeup, hairstyle, and clothing. And Esther completely obeyed the eunuch because the eunuch knew what the king preferred. The eunuch gained nothing from her except the satisfaction of doing his job. After Esther met the king, we never hear about the eunuch again.

Application for Leaders

Just like the eunuch, we who are in authority of leadership must prepare the body of Christ to meet the King. Simply, your job as a leader is to prepare the people under you to be with Jesus. Your authority is simply that God made you with the capability of being a leader and advancing His Kingdom, but it's not about you. It is your job to know the King the best so you can share His heart and prepare His people.

I knew a minister with a successful ministry who ruined it because he thought it was all about him once he started to taste success. Abraham Lincoln said it perfectly, "If you want to test a man's character, give him power." Give a minister or leader success, and you'll see who he really is. Give him numbers, give him people, give him powerful sermons, give him the Holy Spirit, and you'll really see his heart in that moment.

Because it all belongs to God, we are called to steward the ministry God has called us to build. A pastor friend said, "The Lord did not ask you to build His house. He said *He* would build His house. He didn't ask you to do anything, but you can come alongside Him as He builds His house."

The greatest leaders of authority should be the greatest servants of authority. If you cannot serve, you cannot lead. If there is no one to serve in the nursery or clean the bathrooms, then it's our responsibility to step in and serve in those areas. If we think that we're too important to do those things, then we'll surely fail. Jesus even served others when he washed the disciples' feet.

Remember that your leadership authority is a gift that points people to love Jesus. Just like the eunuch in the book of Esther, we can use our influence to advance the Kingdom. Just as Jesus encouraged Simon to throw his net on the other side of the boat, we can use our God-given authority with confidence that is both meek and graceful.

The anointing of the Holy Spirit will give you the proper authority as you show honor and respect to others, including those over you and under you. And then you can be sure that the Kingdom, the circle of God's economy, will go well.

Let me pray for you as you submit yourself to God's economy.

Help us today, Lord God, to use our authority and our influence for Your glory. May Your Kingdom be advanced by the leadership You've put on us. May our leadership never be for our own glory, for our own welfare, or for our own advancement. May it only be for Your heart and for the things that please You. We ask today that You would instill in us a system of honor and a recognition of Your economy that we would understand that the Kingdom of God does not advance the way the Kingdom of the world does. We ask that You touch us and help us to understand Your economy and operate in it, Father, so Your Kingdom can advance in our lives and in Your body. Amen!

CHAPTER THREE

The Balancing Act of Leadership

I BELIEVE THAT THE body of Christ is a kitty cat when she's supposed to be a lion. As a leader in ministry, it's my responsibility to build up the body of Christ and to encourage it to serve with a purpose like those Christians in the book of Acts.

The Holy Spirit spoke to me one day and said, "I want you to write a book."

I told the Lord, "You remember that I don't like to read books let alone write books."

But the Lord said, "I want you to do it, and I'm going to give it to you. I'm going to give it to you in its entirety. I'm going to open up the doors for you. I'm going to bring it all to you, and I'm going to use it as a platform to touch a generation of people. I'm going to use it in a way that you could not imagine. I'm going to open up doors with it, and I just want you to obey me."

And I said, "Lord, I'm in. Whatever You say, I'm in."

A couple of months later, I invited a guest speaker to my church. I had never met him before, but he was a man of God who operates in the prophetic. After his sermon, he told me, "I have a word for you. God has given you a book in your heart, and He is going to use it as a platform."

It was the same word God had given me earlier. I knew God was speaking to me about writing a book.

A couple of months after that, a publisher called my church saying he had been led by the Holy Spirit to call. He told the senior pastor, "Hey listen, the Lord spoke to me. There's a book I'm supposed to publish. Are you writing a book?"

The senior pastor said, "I am not, but my associate pastor has talked about God putting a book in her heart."

I came into the office to speak with the publisher.

The publisher was seventy years old and had been in the publishing industry his whole life. Unimpressed by anyone or anything, he told me that he was only looking to honor God. "Look," he said, "I see twenty to thirty manuscripts a day. Everyone thinks they can write. What's your manuscript about?"

Well, I didn't have a manuscript. I told him, "Let me tell you what I'm about. Let me start there." I shared who I was and what God had called me to do, and that my job in the Kingdom of God was to awaken the body of Christ. I began to share my heart with him, but he interrupted me.

"What's your address?" he asked.

"My address, why?"

He said, "I'm putting a contract in the mail right now. I'm in."

I was shocked. "You haven't seen anything yet!"

He said, "I don't need to see anything. I hear it, and I'm in."

He mailed me the contract. So I had a contract and a deadline, but no book. He wanted the manuscript in a couple of weeks, and I had nothing. I just knew what the Lord had put in my heart, so I spent the next week fasting and praying. I said, "Lord, You put this in my heart. You have to bring it to pass."

The Lord simply said to me, "Daughter, you already wrote it." I love when God speaks to me like that.

The moment God said that, it was as if the scales fell from my eyes. I opened my desk and found journal entries and sermons I had written. I assembled them into a manuscript, made necessary rewrites, and submitted it to the publisher. Within eight months from talking with him on the phone, I had the published book in my hands. God did all the work.

In the midst of that, I had called Cablevision to switch my cable. The gentleman on the phone only had my first name and my address. After he finished the job, he said to me, "I need to ask you a question. Are you a pastor?"

"I am. How do you know that?" I said.

"Because the Holy Spirit's speaking to me about you right now. And God has put a book in your heart."

So God gave me the word for the third time. The third time!

I was completely blown away by what the Lord had done. People have asked me if it was my dream to write a book. No. Writing a book was never my dream and certainly never something I even thought about. The Holy Spirit birthed it and did all the work. And within a month of the book's release date it hit number one on Amazon. I called the publisher and told him.

He said, "You know what? This is unbelievable because I've published books for forty years, and I've never seen this. It's nothing short of the favor of God because you're a no one."

I love that. I'll be a no one for Jesus any day of the week. So that's the premise of my heart. As a leader, I believe God has called me to encourage the body of Christ to live courageously. The days of mediocrity in Christianity need to end. Furthermore, I believe we leaders have been called to lead with courage.

Godly, courageous leadership is a huge passion of my heart. I believe the church is lacking godly leadership. We have managers instead of leaders, and there's a distinct difference. Managers can organize, but leaders inspire others and create more leaders.

Most of the time, leaders don't understand that leadership is a gift and an anointing. We need the anointing of God in order to lead well. Part of leading well is understanding this concept of authority and honor. Leaders need to live by balancing both things. One of the greatest tools to equip us to lead well is what I call a velvet hammer.

The Velvet Hammer of Authority

As a leader, our job is to walk well with the authority we have been given. If the only thing that comes to mind when you think of authority is wielding power, then something is wrong with your authority structure. Does power come with authority? Absolutely. But it should barely be on our authority radar. If you have to walk into a room and tell people you're in charge, you're probably not in charge. In children's workers training, I tell them that the second they raise their voice and tell the kids, "I'm the teacher here," is the second they have lost control, and they are no longer in charge. They have acted upon their authority by using only power. Authority does have power, but the true component of authority is the ability to use that authority to empower others.

A person who's truly in charge is so because they empower others. Authority in leadership should be like what I call a velvet hammer. When you go to the store and purchase a hammer, you're not buying the hammer because you might be mugged in the streets one day and need it as a defense weapon. No. You're buying the hammer because you need to build or fix something. The main purpose of the hammer as well as the main purpose of authority is to empower, to build, to fix. We're given authority to equip and empower the body of Christ and anyone who comes in contact with us. That's true authority. Will you have to correct or rebuke with your authority one day? Sure, but that should be a rare thing!

Jesus is the perfect example of authority. Everywhere He went He empowered, He encouraged, He stretched, and He challenged people. In at least 75 percent of Jesus's miracles in the Bible, He first pulls something out of the person he was dealing with. He doesn't say yes right away. He told the woman with a sick child, "I can't give the children's food to the dogs."

Although it may appear that he insulted her, He actually pulled something out of the woman because she responded, "But even the dogs get crumbs."

He said, "There it is. There it is" (Matt. 15:26–28, author's paraphrase). He taught a lesson that we are still learning today because His authority wasn't a hammer of aggression, it was a velvet hammer that He used gently, He used it properly. He knew when to use it and when not to use it

Because we are supposed to be able to empower, to strengthen, to equip, and to build up others, we add to that empowerment what I call a relational bank.

Relational Bank

I believe that if a leader always operates with force, something is wrong with his or her leadership. We should always operate out of what I call a relational bank. Think of a relational bank as you would think of a bank account. As we develop our leadership skills, we're developing people around us and making deposits into a relational bank. Every relationship, every moment, and every person we meet is an investment.

Many of the churches I minister in have known me for years. Because of that, we have a huge relational bank together. We've worked together, and each time there is an investment in a relational bank that's been built through trust and time. As leaders and as people in authority, we should always operate from a place of relationship. Relationship is found throughout Scripture, and Jesus shows again and again how to build those relationships with people. Consider the relationship of Mary, Martha, and Lazarus. Or the relationship within the disciples. Jesus takes time to invest in these relationships.

As a leader, your authority comes from that place of building relationships. We should be building relationships with those under us and those in higher authority over us.

When it comes to investing in the stock market, it is not a true investment without the word *risk*. As leaders, our investment in people is no different. There is still that risk we take to make the investment, to build the relationship. At one point in my life, I walked through a difficult season with one of my leaders. At first, I started out as his pastor, and then I became his mentor, so we already had an established relationship bank. Eventually I became his boss. We got along fine for the first year and a half. I never had to operate as his boss. I was always his mentor and his pastor. But then something happened.

The more I continued to operate as mentor and pastor and tried to teach, to equip, and to encourage, the more he began to absorb his own relational bank. He changed; he got puffed up, and he became arrogant. Soon that relationship bank ran dry.

Then the only hat I could possibly wear with him was a boss's hat. It's the one that brought correction as well as understanding. Unfortunately, he would not yield, and it ended badly. That was an eight-year investment for me, and it failed. Just because one investment doesn't work does not mean I stop investing in people. People are worth the investment; don't let some bad returns stop you from investing. There will be failures, but the wins will always out number them.

Remember, if we are truly empowering people, we are always working ourselves out of a job. We are always investing in others, and those coming up behind us, to take over our ministry someday, or to allow us to take on more ministry as others are able to fill in wherever they can serve best. The Sunday morning that runs flawlessly without you is the day you have done your job as a leader. We don't like to think about possibly losing our job security, but once we understand that building and equipping people allows for even more ministry to happen, then we know that we are doing the right thing. God gives you more as you empower more people, as you send them out on their own to serve in the ministry, then God gives you more opportunities to invest and empower. Authority used properly in this way releases people in the ministry. This kind of authority allows them to make mistakes, and they're not afraid of your response.

The Hammer of Protection

Sometimes in our leadership, we have to use the velvet hammer to bring correction, to bring encouragement, to bring empowerment. But at times leaders operate under that hard hammer of protection. This is especially true when someone is out to hurt those who are in our ministry. We must use the hard hammer to protect and defend. God's entrusted the people in our ministry to us, and to use the hard hammer is to act under righteous authority. There are some leaders, though, who do not operate that hard hammer with righteousness.

I had a young man join my church and start a young adults ministry. His former leader had been a hard-hammer leader. On this young man's first day with me, he sat in my office, trembling. He said, "I know you want me to build this, but can you tell me the parameters?"

I grabbed his hand and said, "I'm going to start with one sentence. You can fail at this."

He said, "What?"

I said, "You can absolutely fail at this."

"What do you mean?" he asked.

I said, "I'm telling you that you can mess this up, and I'm okay with it because I know your intention is not to mess it up. So, you do your best. If it works, it works. If it fails, it fails, but we'll work together."

Something happened in that boy's heart because the pastor before me was all hammer, all the time, and he was not allowed to make a mistake. You know what happened to the ministry he built under me? It skyrocketed. You know why? Because he was encouraged that he could try, he could hear God, and there could be room for failure too.

Because of the encouragement of my leadership and not operating under hard-hammer authority, this young man grew in leadership and in the ministry he served. We need to allow room for failure because in that failure, people learn, grow, and succeed. I am sorry if you have experienced poor leadership authority. If you've sat under authority that's been like a hammer in your life, I'm sorry that happened. We can indeed learn to operate not under the hard hammer of leadership but begin to operate under that velvet hammer of authority and empower others to learn, grow, and lead. By working with others in the right way, we can encourage and develop people so that they can, in turn, develop others. We build each other to build the ministry. When people serve under your protection and feel that you will have their back you have now taken the lid off their ministry and yours.

Developing People While on the Job

As we begin to walk in the things of God and begin to understand what authority looks like from His perspective, authority is one of the coolest responsibilities because you can watch how people develop. Our role as a leader is crucial to those who are under us, to those who are simply around us, and to those we are helping to develop to take over different parts of the ministry.

There was a young girl who served with me at a church who is now a children's pastor at another church. There are eight hundred people in her church, and the children's department is huge. She runs it with grace, mercy, and right thinking. She's clear in what she understands. Everybody's talking about this young lady and how she just came out of nowhere.

But she didn't come out of nowhere. She is successful in what she does because of years of time and investment. She was an investment in years of planting, investing, giving, encouraging, and building. That's not to my credit, but to God's credit. That's what good authority looks like.

When this young lady was under my leadership, one area she hated was confrontation.

I said, "Me too. No one likes to confront people, but I need you to learn how to do it."

"But I'm shy," she said.

I told her we'd pray about that, and as we did, we kept moving forward.

She eventually grew out of her shyness and learned how to confront people. I would teach her that as a leader you have to learn how to call people out on their junk, she would say, "Yeah, but I don't like doing that."

I replied, "I don't like 90 percent of my job sometimes, but I have to do it. That's what I'm called to do."

If I am not able to empower people with gentle confrontation in love, then what is my purpose in the body of Christ?

I told her, "If I'm not going to stand behind you and push you forward, then my authority is for nothing."

Throughout the time I was with her, I was near enough to protect her, near enough to hear her if she needed me, and near enough to guide her if she went a little bit too far. I worked with and mentored her for many years. As her leader, I poured my life into her, and when I stepped back, she blossomed and was able to confidently run the children's department. She grew into this area so well that now everyone sees the fruit. Good authority in leadership challenges, develops, encourages, and empowers others, which always produces the better results in the ministry.

Developing People While on Vacation

Sometimes we are called to develop people even while we are on vacation. We never stop being leaders.

I was on a cruise vacation a few years back. One day I was relaxing in the pool, and I caught the conversation of twenty people also in the pool talking about their churches. Immediately I thought it was a setup from God, so I continued to listen to their complaints about church. One person didn't go to church anymore because the pastor was a crook. Another didn't attend church because their pastor did this or that. Another's pastor was unfaithful.

As they talked, I was listening, and I said in my heart, "Lord, if you open the door, I'll walk in." And I waited for an opportunity.

One of the guys in the group turned around to me and said, "What do you think?" There was twenty people in the pool, and he turns to me!

Right there, I realized this was a platform, an opportunity to empower others. I said, "You probably don't go to the doctor, do you?"

He said, "Of course, we go to doctors."

I said, "Well, did you ever have a bad doctor?"

"Of course we did."

"So, when you had a bad doctor, did that stop you from pursuing good health? You kept looking until you found a doctor who worked for you, is that correct?"

And they all said, "Yeah."

And I said, "So why did you give up on God because of bad pastors? Why didn't you keep looking until you found a pastor who spoke to your heart and ministered to you?"

They froze, and I said, "Yeah, see that's the thing. You guys have thrown out God because of poor representation." They were all in shock, and I was thanking the Lord for His wisdom.

Then one of the guys asked me what I did for a living.

I started laughing and said, "I'm a pastor," and they all laughed too. I said to them, "It is not by chance or coincidence that I'm standing here right now at this moment. This is God speaking to you guys, all of you. God orchestrated my time so that I'm here right now to tell you that it's time to start seeking Him again."

Then the most amazing thing happened. I asked each one of them where they lived. Being on a cruise ship, people come from all over. As each one of them told me where they lived, I told them I knew a pastor and a church near each of them. I was able to plug each of them into a good church with a good pastor-leader. As I sat there soaking up the sun in that pool, I said, "God, You're amazing."

If we're open to it, God will use us in the right moments of authority to lead, encourage, strengthen, and empower others in their own lives and ministries. Authority and leadership don't just happen within the church. Authority happens when we walk outside the doors. We have the authority of Christ wherever we walk, even in a pool on a Royal Caribbean cruise.

Application for Leaders

As we operate in the authority God has given us, we can pull people into a relationship with the Lord Jesus Christ. In a culture that may seem harsh at times, we can always lead with grace and courage because we are not supposed to operate under the culture out there. We're not meant to be afraid of the culture; we are meant to change it. If we steer the culture of the church with a velvet hammer when necessary and always seek to love and empower others, then we will build people and our ministries well.

CHAPTER FOUR

Gifts Are Free, Character Is Expensive

BEFORE WE CAN GO any further, it's important that we understand the desire to change. As leaders, we should want to be changed. And if you don't want to be changed, then adjust because we need to want to be changed. We need to want to be different. We need to want to grow. Growth has some pain and some pressure, but that's the only way it's done. No one grows by wishing; you grow by being intentional. Now, let's talk about growing, moving, changing, and understanding that God wants to do work in us. May it be our desire to let God speak to us in this matter of change and growth so we can be the vessel God wants us to be.

September 1, 2018, kicked off my twenty-eighth year in pastoral ministry. I had first started in Bible school as a teen. I love the ministry and the things of God. I love watching God, big, bold, and on display. I love watching the gifts of the Holy Spirit. I love watching people get healed, delivered, and set free.

I bleed to see transformation happen. That's my DNA. I was raised in a Pentecostal setting, and I am Pentecostal through and through.

I love watching God show off. It's kind of like saying, "That's my dad. You see what He does? That's how He works." I love watching people walk in sick and walk out delivered. I love watching God heal broken marriages in one sentence. I love watching prophetic words that cut to the bone and marrow and transform someone's life. I've seen all those things.

Someone asked me once, "Why is it every time you preach, you share a miracle?" And I thought that was such a strange question because it has a simple answer: I serve a current God. I don't serve a God that *did*, I serve a God that *does* and *continues to do*, so I want to put Him on display. I want the world to know God is active, and He's moving.

Using Our Gifts and Developing Our Character

When we see the gifts in operation, and God shifting things through the gifts, and people in the body of Christ stepping out and using them, we are watching people leading in a sweet spot in the Kingdom. As leaders, we see people use those gifts tremendously: incredible teachers, preachers, people who lay hands on the sick and the sick recover, and others who prophesy. It is amazing to witness! It has been a joy for me to see.

But there's something else I've seen that is quite sobering. Those same leaders crash, burn, and fall on their faces. Perhaps you can think of someone in ministry who has fallen flat. These are people we consider leadership gurus, leaders we look up to as teachers and preachers. Yet they have these terrible secret lives.

How is it possible to be used so tremendously in the gifts, so powerfully in healing, deliverance, teaching, preaching, and all these other things, and yet they have sin in their lives? How can the gifts and the sin reside in the same place? It is very simple. A gift is free, but character is expensive.

We think that because someone's gifted, his or her character is in line. We think that the gifting and character walk side by side. Rather, a gift is simply given, and character is developed. Someone can sing or preach, so we put them on the platform. Another person can teach, so we put them in a classroom. Just because someone is gifted doesn't mean they have their house in order, and it doesn't mean they can lead.

God loves people. If there is someone riddled with cancer, God wants to heal that person, and the vessel He uses is irrelevant. It could even be a dirty vessel. He loves that person and will heal that person through whatever vessel is present. In the Old Testament, God used a donkey to speak for Him. Don't think He doesn't use donkeys in the New Testament as well.

We mistake gifts for character in the Kingdom. We think that they go together, but they don't. Gifts are given, but character comes from being intentional. I choose to have godly character. I choose to be like Jesus. I choose, and I decide to follow after Him. I decide to walk after Him. I decide to bring my life in subjection to Him. That's how character is developed. It comes from an intentional place. It doesn't come by chance. It doesn't come by wishing. True, godly character comes from choosing to be intentional.

We talk about people having a gift and their character not being developed, and Jesus spoke of the same thing in Matthew, chapter 7: "Many will say to Me in that day, 'Lord, Lord, have we not prophesied in Your name, cast out demons in Your name, and done many wonders in Your name?' And then I will declare to them, 'I never knew you; depart from Me, you who practice lawlessness!'" (Matt. 7:22–23).

What a terrifying statement that is! It should make every believer and leader tremble. What they're saying is, "Lord, I was used in the gifts. I cast out demons. I worked. I was used in the healing. I did all these things in Your name." Because they were depending only on their gifts, He had to cast them out. The gifts by themselves are not enough, which is where we need to understand the difference between *gifts* and *anointing*.

The Difference between Gifts and Anointing

A gift is given. I give my friend a gift, and he receives it. But anointing comes from another place. An anointing comes from sitting with Jesus because *anointing* literally translates: Jesus rubbed up and is smearing on you so that you reflect Him. Literally, he rubs off on you! That only comes from being in His presence. That only comes from a life surrendered to Him. That only comes from the place where you sit at His feet as He does work in you. That's where anointing comes from. It doesn't come from any other place.

As He does that work in you, this anointed life in which you are now allowing Him to speak, to reflect, to wash, and to clean is being refined. You're surrendering, and each place that you surrender, more anointing comes. Now, if we can get the gifts and the anointing to work together, we have the life God wants us to have. We have what we call an open Heaven.

Because as you surrender your life, Heaven will open even more. There's more room for Him to fill. But if there is too much of you present, there's not enough room for Him to fill. He kind of finds His way, but that's not His best. Ultimately, God wants leaders who reflect Him in their leadership, leaders He can rub up against, and leaders who sit at His feet daily.

In fact, in Acts, chapter 4, when Peter and John are arrested, the Sanhedrin begins to question them. The Bible says the Sanhedrin was "marveled by these unlearned, uneducated fishermen" (Acts 4:13, author's paraphrase). Why? Because Peter and John looked like Jesus. They had been in His presence, and now they resembled Him. They were anointed. God is looking for leaders to anoint, but that anointing comes at a cost.

Second Corinthians 7:1 says, "Therefore, having these promises, beloved, let us cleanse ourselves from all filthiness of the flesh and spirit, perfecting holiness in the fear of God." Again. "Therefore, having these promises, beloved, let us cleanse ourselves from all filthiness of the flesh and spirit, perfecting holiness in the fear of God."

We have all these promises—the gifts such as deliverance, healing, freedom, and righteousness—so let us cleanse ourselves from all filth of the flesh and the spirit, perfecting holiness in the fear of God. God wants us to lead with intentionality, and that means to make sure our lives are in order according to what God wants. He will help us perfect His holiness, but we must do the work and daily walk with Him. As we daily walk after being like Jesus, we must daily evaluate our lives. We can't be the leaders of character He has called us to be or live anointed lives without being intentional about doing these things.

I always hear that time matures one's character, but time doesn't mature anyone, nor does it build character. Time exposes character. I love when one of my spiritual daughters say that they've found their husband after only knowing them three weeks. You know what my answer always is? Give it time! Why? Because time will always show character. Time never matured anyone, it simply exposes. As a leader, I must remind them to give it time because that will show a person's true character. Pressure also reveals a person's character. Couple time and pressure, and true character will be revealed.

Maturity and character are intentional because we need to determine to have godly character and to be the leader God wants us to be. We make it our business to keep our lives aligned to God. We make it our business to become like Jesus and to bring our lives under His lordship. There's intentionality in that. Leadership doesn't happen by chance, time, or anything else. Leadership is intentional work on our part as a child of God.

Compartments

Leader, I want to introduce you to a word, and that word is *compartment*. Think of compartments like the dented surface of a waffle. I love to watch my nephews pour syrup in every single compartment, and they don't want any of it to overflow into an adjacent square. I don't know how they think that's not going to happen, but everyone has their own way of eating waffles. But that's a little bit like how we're made. Some of us are better at managing a lot of things, and some of us are terrible at it. The majority of us, however, work in compartments.

When we go to work, that's our work compartment. When we play, that's our play compartment. When we plan, we're in our planning compartment. We get in the zone in each compartment. Sometimes, people live in those compartments, and that can be fine, but that can also be dangerous because if we have compartments no one can touch, then we have compartments no one can correct, including the Holy Spirit. There shouldn't be any compartment in your life, leader, that Jesus can't touch.

Sometimes we have those areas, those compartments in our lives that belong to only us, that we don't want anyone else to know about. Not even God. Those secret compartments are ours and no one else's. But when we became a child of God and especially when we became a leader, we gave up words like *me* and *mine*. All those little things we don't think are a big deal become a big deal because if they're not touchable, then they can't be cleaned. And now that compartment becomes a secret life.

One of my childhood best friends had been in ministry a long time. He was pastoring a church, and for three years of that pastorate, he was having an affair with a woman in the church. This discovery brought the church to its knees. My pastor friend was pulled out of the ministry. When we had a chance to talk a couple of months later, I asked him for understanding of this devastating situation. He explained that it was his Tuesday compartment. He said, "All six other days I was pastor, and I did my job well. I prayed, and I preached, and I ministered. I sang and worshiped, and did all I had to do, but Tuesday, that was my deal."

It's terrifying how we can operate our lives that way, or that we can lead in that way, but we can. We can do everything right except for this little area over here. However, this is a reckless way to live. As a leader, we need to be on point everywhere. We can't have a Tuesday compartment or a Wednesday compartment. We can't have a six o'clock compartment or a two a.m. compartment. Everything about our ministry and what we do must be subject to Jesus and what He has for us.

Your compartment may be something as small as watching a questionable television show and isn't anywhere near as bad as my pastor friend's compartment. Yet, we need to be vigilant to make sure that our compartments are vulnerable and open for anyone to look inside.

Ephesians 5:3 (NIV) says, "But among you there must not even be a hint of sexual immorality, any type of impurity or greed because these things are improper for God's holy people." God is setting a standard for holy leaders. He desires for these things not to be found in us not even a hint. But if these things are present, we must begin to clean house. We can't wait until the house is a hot mess to start cleaning.

For example, years ago in the book *America's Last Call*, author David Wilkerson approached an evangelist and said, "I had a vision of you, and there was a snake by your feet, and you could step on it." The evangelist received the word. A couple years later David Wilkerson approached him again and said, "Sir, I had the same vision of you. The snake was up to your shoulders, but you can strangle it. Kill it." The evangelist simply nodded and did nothing. Then a few years later, Wilkerson saw him again and said, "I had the same vision. Now the snake is all over you, but the Lord will still give you strength. You have a year to kill the snake." And a year later, that man's whole ministry crumbled to the ground. He had been having multiple affairs and lived a wretched lifestyle.[2]

Leader, you have to kill the snake, right there, when there is just a hint.

We must be a people who are willing to be honest and help us take care of all the little compartments in our lives that don't bring Him glory. We need to bring it all under submission to Him. Many times, we make excuses for our actions. We might say, "That's just how I was raised." However, as followers of Jesus, we have to get under the blood of Jesus because we have a new life, a new Father, and a new bloodline. We must bring every compartment of our lives under subjection to the lordship of Jesus because that's the only way we're going to live under an open Heaven. That's the only way Heaven is going to open over you where the anointing drips on your life. He will not give His anointing to the broken house of our lives. He'll give gifts, but He won't give the anointing. And I don't want the gifts without the anointing because I want the anointing and the gifts to go together.

When We Ignore Our Compartments

I had the privilege of speaking at the United Nations. Coming from an immigrant background, it was a tremendous honor for me. Speaking to two hundred Christians who work

---

2. David Wilkerson, *America's Last Call* (New Kensington, PA: Whitaker House, 2000).

at the United Nations reminded me of the book of Acts with people of every nationality, color, creed, and language. At the end, I got to pray for people, and I prayed for this woman who was having brain scans because she was in so much pain. It's one of the few times in my life that the prayer was like ping-pong; it hit a wall and came right back to me.

I sensed some issues going on, so I mentioned them to her. She admitted she had unforgiveness toward her boss and didn't want to forgive him.

I said, "Then I got nothing to pray with you about. We're done."

She was surprised I wouldn't pray for healing for her. I told her I couldn't because Scripture was clear on the need to forgive in order for healing to take place. The compartment of unforgiveness didn't allow Heaven to be open for her.

She said, "I'm going to take your word into consideration."

I told her I thought she was going to reason herself into her unforgiveness.

And oftentimes, like this woman, that's what we do. We reason ourselves into our compartments. We reason ourselves into all kinds of things, and we end up being bound by them. Therefore, we are unable to be effective leaders, but we don't have to stay that way. We can deal with each compartment of our lives and make sure that everything is properly taken care of so that we can be the effective leaders God has called us to be for the ministries we serve.

I had the same story unfold in Africa years later. A woman walked into the church where I was preaching, and she was having a stroke. Her entire left side was paralyzed. I ran to her and asked if she needed to go the hospital. She had just left there. She had no money, so they would not help her. She came to the church for prayer. I began to pray, and again it felt like a ping-pong; my pray never left the room. I asked her if there was any unforgiveness in her heart, and she said yes. I told her that if she wanted to be healed, she had to forgive. She did! She wept and wept, but she forgave. Right after, I prayed again for healing, my prayer felt like a rocket! Immediately she was completely healed! Heaven opened over her!

Application for Leaders

As leaders serving others and God in the ministries we are called to, we must bring our affections, our lives, our dreams, and our desires before the Lord because He requires a life completely surrendered to Him.

Christine Caine, in several of her sermons, says we should allow God to work deeply in us so He can work powerfully through us. Leader, allow God to work deeply in you so He can work powerfully through you. If you want God to flow in and through your ministry, be willing to do the work and dig into those deep compartments of your life and allow Him to work deeply in you.

To let God work deeply in us, we must desire the change to take place and adjust our lives. We need to want to grow, but all growth has some pain in it. And growth has some pressure, but that's the only way we grow. We don't grow by wishing. We grow only by being intentional. As we are intentional about making sure our lives align with God and adjust the compartments in our lives, then we can begin to ask God for an open

Heaven. And we can begin to ask Him for the anointing and for His Spirit to be poured over us and over our ministry.

And then we become anointed people, ready for the Master's hand. Ready for Him to use us the way He needs to. Godly leadership comes when the anointing and the gifts match. And then we become unstoppable as effective leaders for Christ.

CHAPTER FIVE

Leading through the Winter

EACH NEW YEAR'S DAY I ask God to give me a portion of Scripture for the year. At one point of my life for three years in a row, God gave me Habakkuk 3:17–19. I would love to tell you that when I got this verse I was overjoyed with God. I was not. I wanted Jeremiah 29:11 or one of those rejoicing kinds of verses. Habakkuk 3:17–19 was not that; however, these verses, to me, have become very personal.

When God gave me these verses, I said, "God, what are you saying?"

He said, "It's going to be a winter season, but I'm going to teach you to lead in the winter season." And He did for years.

The verses go like this: "Though the fig tree may not blossom, nor the fruit be on the vines, though the labor of the olive may fail, and the fields yield no fruit, though the flock may be cut off from the fold, and there be no herd in the stalls—yet I will rejoice in the Lord. I will rejoice in the God of my salvation. The Lord God is my strength; he will make my feet like deer's feet, and He will make me walk on my high hills." In these verses, there's no fruit. There are no animals. There's no water. There's nothing. God is saying, "It's going to be a barren season. It's going to be a cold season."

Before I take these verses apart for us, I want us to understand the concept of spiritual seasons. Our walk with God and our walk in leadership has seasons much like earthly seasons. There is the summer season everyone loves; everything is light, easy, bright, things are simple, and you are good with life. Ministry feels good, and you can see the hand of God in everything. The spring season is all about new birth and things coming to life; new ideas are popping up, and God's voice is rich. The fall is all about change, different colors, different experiences. It feels a little cooler, but change is in the air; you can kind of sense what God is doing. The winter is cold, barren, seemingly empty. God seems very far; His voice seems to be nowhere, and everything feels dead. How many times have you walked through a cold, barren winter in your ministry? How many know what winter feels like when you're walking with the Lord, and it feels as if nothing seems to be alive? Things die in the winter. Things die off because it's cold, and it's barren, and there's no sunlight. For all of its seemingly deadness, the winter season, out of all the other seasons, is the most important. Because this season, when things seem barren, when things seem dry, when things seem like they're dying, is when you are planting the most. And as a leader you must lead strong in the winter.

Regardless of the season, you're always planting. It's really easy to plant and to speak faith and grace when there's sunlight. It's easy to be kind when everything is wonderful. It's easy for the world to look at us when things are going great. It's easy because we're full of joy and peace. It is easy to lead then; everyone is good.

It's the winter season, when things aren't going well, when things aren't the way we anticipated, then it is easy to get discouraged and lose heart. However, we must fight against it. Because this dark season is when leaders plant the most. In this season where there are no figs and no oil and no cattle, where things look empty and barren, I am planting the most seed. How do I have joy when things seem to be failing? What is my response to the winter season? How do I move forward and lead in the winter so people can follow my example?

We all have heard of this concept of seasons that we will walk through because we are leaders and Christians. We all love the spring and summer seasons. We don't even mind the fall season. But it's the winter season that's difficult. The winter season is the one we hear the least about because it's the least favorable. No one wants the winter season. We want the sunshine. We want the seasons of harvest. The winter season is rough because the winter season is dark, cold, lifeless, fruitless, and difficult to lead through. Sometimes we will have to lead through difficult times, and we must lead well. The question is, how do we lead well when everything around us looks bad?

We must realize something that will help us greatly in the winter seasons. It is in that season that God is trying to remove things in our lives or in our ministries. Winter exposes and allows us to see who we really are, and we begin to see who He's trying to shape us to be. The winter causes the façades to fall off and shows us where we have fallen short and where we need to grow. Winter also reveals areas yet to be planted. It shows the strength and weakness of our leadership because all the pretense has been removed, and only the real person remains. I call that the darkroom of winter.

The Darkroom of Winter

The winter season is like processing film in a darkroom. We walk around taking pictures with our cell phones, but some of us from the ice age remember something called film. You load the camera with film and take all the pretty pictures you want. However, with film, we don't get the picture right away. It has to be processed in a darkroom. The film goes through ten processes in that darkroom, and if you open the door before all the processes are done, the picture is ruined. Like processing film, God gives us a picture of what He has for us, but then, because He loves us and wants us to grow and mature in our leadership, He puts us in a darkroom so we will walk through the process of developing, the process of growth, the process of death, the process of dying to self, the process of letting things go. And when the time is right and He opens the door, the picture He took and the picture we see are the same.

During those winter seasons, if we're not careful, we can forget why we're there. We can forget why God is walking us through them. We wonder why God allows this to happen in our lives and why things are not happening the way we wanted. Why is this experience so painful? Why are our dreams not materializing? We ask God why things aren't working out the way we thought they should?

It's in that season that God is trying to remove the things that are not like Him. That's really what the winter season is for. It's in that season that we better know that the joy of the Lord is our strength. We better understand that we are leaning on the character of who God is because it's His character that we rest on. It's His Word that we trust. If I can see, why do need trust or faith? When I can't see is when God's character and His Word had better be close.

Just as children do something that gives them a boo-boo, which hopefully teaches them to not do it again, God puts us through the darkroom of pain that teaches us and shapes us. We don't like the discomfort that the pain of winter brings, but pain is necessary for growth. Through the trials of our lives, we find the ugly is transformed into something beautiful just like winter transforms into spring and spring into summer.

The place of deep learning is the winter. The place of testing is the winter. The place of growth, whether you feel it or not, is the winter—that place where there are no figs, no oil, no water, and no animals. That's where the rubber meets the road, and you begin to understand either He is God or He is not God, whether He is true or not true, whether He is faithful or not faithful. It's in those dark moments of winter that you find out exactly who God is and you walk with Him. You allow Him to kill off the things that are not like Him so that when the darkroom door opens, the picture of your leadership matches God and His Word. Leader, you can never lead anyone through the winter if all you know is the summer.

Surrendering in the Winter Season

When I walked through this season with the Lord, I said, "Lord, I feel like I'm dying." You know what He said to me? He said, "So just die and stop fighting. Just yield. I'm trying to kill something. Let it die." Why would He say something like that? Because only when something truly dies, can something else truly live.

Growing up, I attended the High School of Performing Arts, the school that the TV program, *Fame*, was based on. When I graduated, I wanted to be a Broadway actress. Oh, and I wanted to also be a preacher and to practice law. Somehow I was going to do all three. Right before graduation, we had a talent showcase in front of famous directors and school representatives. They were offering scholarships to the best drama colleges and universities in the country; NYU was the most sought after one. I finished my showcase, and I was offered the NYU scholarship! I was elated to fulfill my dream, and I could not wait to share with my friends from church.

As I left school and walked by Lincoln Center in New York City, thinking and planning out my life, the Holy Spirit said very gently, "Did you ask me if you could go?"

I said, "No. You might say no." I walked a little farther then stopped right by the fountain. "Lord, can I go?"

He said, "No. That's not what I have for you. I have something else. Would you do what I have for you?"

I paused, considering how much I really wanted to go into Broadway acting. I had my whole life planned out; this was a chance of a lifetime! Then I said, "Lord, my life is yours. I gave it to you. You get to instruct it any way that You want." I gave back that scholarship. Everyone thought I was completely out of my mind. But I obeyed God, and I walked a completely different path than what I had planned.

And from what I have experienced since, no Broadway stage performance could ever give me the joy and the life I've seen throughout my ministry. I've seen thousands of people give their lives to Jesus. I've seen blind eyes opened. I've seen the lame walk. I've seen God move with power. The sacrifice I thought I was making was nothing compared to what He gave back to me. Something had to die for something else to live because He has a better plan for me.

Allowing the Potter to Shape Us

As we walk through winter seasons, God is trying to shape us, fashion us, and develop us to be more like Jesus. It's painful, and it's harsh. Just like the picture He took of our lives and the picture that's eventually developed, if we give up on the process and open the door, that film is ruined, and God has to start again.

Another way to see this is through the potter's wheel in Jeremiah: "The word which came to Jeremiah from the Lord saying: 'Arise and go down to the potter's house, and there I will cause you to hear my words.' Then I went down to the potter's house, and there he was, making something at the wheel. But the vessel that he made of clay was marred in the hand of the potter; so he made it again into another vessel, as it seemed good to the potter to make" (Jer. 18:1–4).

Each leader is on the potter's wheel at some point. God molds us and shapes us. Sometimes flaws happen. Scripture refers to that as, "marred in the hand of the potter." Something goes wrong. Maybe air gets into the clay causing bubbles that weaken it.

One of the biggest problems in Haiti is that their buildings are made of limestone, a very cheap building material. That's why if something hits them, it all falls apart. The consistency of what they build with is not strong enough. Limestone looks strong, but it is filled with air.

As the potter works on a piece of clay, air gets in it, and the piece is marred. It's not strong enough. Instead of continuing to build that defective piece of pottery, the potter starts all over again. Why? Because he wants to make it strong. He wants to make it last. He wants to make it so that when something blows against it, when something pushes against it, even when it's dropped, it'll stand. The Scripture says, "He made it again into another vessel." Did you catch that word? It was something different than what he started with. He made it into *another* vessel. It was good in the potter's hands.

Leader, as we walk through life, we run into all kinds of deficiencies. We get air bubbles all over the place that make us fragile and weak. God wants to work all those things out—everything that doesn't look like Jesus. He wants to take the vessels that we are today and make us into other vessels that are good in the potter's hands so that the potter can look at them and say, "They're ready. They're ready for the next chapter. They're ready for the next page. They're ready for the next challenge. They're ready for whatever's going to come their way because I'm able to fashion them."

Imagine if the clay fought the potter. Imagine if the clay said, "I'm not in. This is too painful. This is too hard. This is too difficult." Salvation is free, but everything else in God requires work. Everything else requires us to say, "I want to grow. I want to be more like Jesus. I want to change." Those winter seasons are when He puts us through that change, and it doesn't feel great. Yet if we will learn to grow in them, if we will learn to plant properly while in them, we'll see the hand of God.

I walked through a winter season for three years, and during that time, I went to Mexico for a vacation. I've learned that even in the winter season God can use us powerfully. When I was traveling back, a gentleman across the aisle from me on the plane said, "My friend is in the bathroom, really sick."

All of a sudden, we heard them calling the tower because we had to make an emergency landing. This friend was *really* sick. I asked the guy what was wrong.

"I think he has E. coli. I think he ate something in Mexico he shouldn't have eaten. He's been vomiting all day."

They had this gentleman laid out. He was green. He was trembling and shaking. Someone called for any medical personnel on the plane to come and help. They're talking with the tower trying to figure out what to do.

I said, "Lord, what do you want me to do?"

The Lord said, "Go pray for him."

I got up from my seat and got right next to the young man. "Sir, can I pray for you?"

"Please, please."

I laid my hands on him, and I prayed out loud. Everyone was respectful. I finished praying, went to my seat, and started to minister to his friend. Then within an hour or so, they came to him and said, "Your friend took a turn. His color's back. He's sitting up. He's not vomiting anymore."

The man across the aisle looked at me and said, "It's because we prayed, right?"

Even though I was in a winter season of my life, ministry, and leadership, I was able to minister to this sick young man and have an effective influence on others.

Application for Leaders

During the winter darkroom season in our leadership, we must walk with faith, confidence, and strength because God is with us, and others are watching. If God be for me, who can be against me? Even when we can't see, it doesn't matter because God sees. Will we trust Him in those dark places and trust what He sees and that He understands?

One of my favorite verses is found in the book of Acts when Peter and John were arrested. They were brought before the Sanhedrin when someone said something very simple: "These are uneducated, unlearned men, but they look like Jesus" (Acts 4:13, author's paraphrase). It wasn't that their physical face looked like Jesus; it's that they resembled Jesus. They sounded like Jesus.

How beautiful would it be if as we're walking through dark places, we look and sound more like Jesus and love more like Jesus. Each day we're being shaped into His image. And when spring, fall, and summer come, we can enjoy the fruit of what we planted in the winter. One season feeds three seasons if we plant properly. Hear that again: one season feeds three seasons if we plant properly.

If you allow Him to, God will shape and fashion you into the image of Jesus each day. He will transform you into the leader He has called you to be no matter the season. If you will trust Him, you will never have to fear the winter again.

Here is a prayer for you as you go through the winter season:

Lord, today I lift up all these leaders who are walking through a winter season. I pray, God, that You give them courage and that they don't lose heart. I pray, God, that You reveal Yourself even in the winter and that You give them peace and strength. I pray they would lead well, that they don't faint, and that they will remember that this one season will feed the next three seasons. Give them grace in Jesus's name!

CHAPTER SIX

Leaders Get Dirty

JOHN MAXWELL SAYS THAT leadership is influence. I like this idea a lot, but to be a good Christian leader, I believe we need a little more. There have been many people, such as Hitler, who have had great influence and a following. But just because someone has influence doesn't mean they are a good leader. Because an ineffective leader can lead people the wrong way, it's important to understand what influence for the people of God must look like.

I love this definition of a leader, also by Maxwell: "A leader is one who knows the way, goes the way, and shows the way." That's the difference for the church. It's not simply about having influence. A leader for the church knows the way, and knows how to get us there. The leader goes the way. That's where we mess up as leaders. We know the way, but we don't necessarily go the way or show others the way.

One of the speakers at a leader's event I attended was Frances Chan, one of the most sought-after speakers of our time. When it was his turn to speak, he had a hard time. He said that his message was about discipleship, and he didn't know if he wanted us making disciples because the rule of discipleship is: "Follow me as I follow Christ." Unless leaders were following Christ, we shouldn't make disciples; it makes everyone else's job harder.

That's where leaders mess up. So this is a really good definition to work with. A leader is someone who knows the way, goes the way, and shows the way. It's three parts. So that adds onto more than just our influence as a leader. I can influence you because I know the way, I'm going the way, and I'm taking you along the way.

What Is Influence?

Influence is a word that requires a lot of work and a lot of understanding. The ability to influence people comes out of this key truth: investment. I cannot truly influence someone's life until I have invested in them. People don't care about where you want to take them until they know you care about them.

There are plenty of leaders who can influence from the podium, but there is a deeper level of influence when you're doing life with them. When you walk with people as a leader, and get dirty with them, it's an investment.

When people feel invested in, you have the ability to speak into anything. They trust you because you're willing to get dirty with them. You're not looking at their dirt and getting afraid or judging them. You're looking at their dirt, saying, "Okay, let's walk the journey together." When we begin to operate on that level, our influence completely changes because that's when we have the ability to influence and influence greatly.

The business of the church is people, and this is where leaders get mixed up because the church is not a program. I have worked at a church with fifteen hundred people. And I always hear questions about how the programs are going. I had to remind my staff that our church is not program-driven; we're here for people. We are in the business of building people. And the church must keep sight of that. The more you grow as a leader, the more you're in the business of building people. You can build systems because we need systems, but the most important thing is to build and influence people.

If you learn to invest in someone then teach that person to invest in someone else and that person teaches the next person to invest, then the church will never lack volunteers, workers, or leaders. But if you're just building systems and programs, you'll run out of people. And all that we've built will die with that generation.

Five Levels of Leadership

I want to borrow from a previous chapter on John Maxwell's five levels of leadership to help you see how important it is to invest in people.

Level 1 is the level of rights or positional leadership. People follow leaders at this level because they have to. Most leaders don't invest in those under them because they just need workers. Leaders have position and the title, so people respect that.

Level 2 is where people follow because they choose to. They believe in you, and they trust you. There's a beginning of relationship there. They like you because you're a good person. You smile. You're friendly. You're warm. That is the beginning of the investment. As a leader, you're starting to step into a greater level of leadership.

Level 3 is production because you have proven results. People follow because of what you have done for the organization or what you have accomplished. People trust your ability to build up others. They trust the organization and how you think. They want to be part of something successful. This is an even greater level of leadership.

Level 4 centers around people development. People follow you because of what you have done for them. This level is the highest level of investment in a person. This leader pours out themselves into others and is a leader-maker.

Level 5 is a leader who is over other leaders like the late Billy Graham was. We are talking about a king, someone who has held a national platform of influence who everyone wants to follow. A level 5 leader status requires nearly a lifetime of proven leadership.

But let's go back to level 4 leadership. We should all desire level 4 leadership because it's the investment in others that counts. People don't walk in pretty or clean shaven, ready to lead. I've had the pleasure of working with hundreds of leaders. Our job as leaders is to find the diamonds and invest in them, clean and polish them. When we invest in others and care for others, the power of that investment is such that they will want to reproduce it. They want to do for somebody else what you've done for them. That's powerful because then a ministry is reproducible. The ministry now becomes like a polished, clear-cut diamond where people understand how to invest in and clean and polish others.

Moses, the Greatest Leader

Moses was the greatest leader in the Old Testament. Hebrews chapter 3 says he was the greatest servant in the house, second only to Jesus, who was lord over the house. But Moses was a hot mess because he had identity issues. He didn't know whether he was Hebrew or Egyptian. He had family problems. He was a murderer and a fugitive. He stuttered and didn't have the ability to speak. What made Moses the greatest leader in the Old Testament?

God began to speak life into him. God said, "Moses, I've called you. I have my hand on your life. I put my word in you; I put my fire in you."

"I can't speak," Moses said.

God said, "I'll send your brother."

"I don't have any power," Moses said.

God said, "Use the stick in your hand, Moses. I won't even change what's in your hand; I'll use what you know, but I'll teach you how to use it properly."

And God kept pouring into Moses. When Moses and Aaron finally went before Pharaoh, Aaron never spoke. Moses did it every time.

So even with the crutch and major issues Moses had, the Bible calls him the greatest servant of the house because God saw in him something He could pull out. And that's the job of a leader: to see something in someone that they often don't see in themselves.

Different Kinds of Investment

Along the way in our ministries, we will have to know how to invest in people according to how they react or respond.

Sometimes we will be able to invest deeply in others. And sometimes we will have to invest slowly.

Incremental Investment: About fourteen years ago, a young lady walked into my office and said she wanted to be a classroom assistant. "Put me in a classroom with the littlest kids. I want to pour juice, and I want to serve cookies. That's all I want to do."

I said that was fine, but I saw something in her that could be more. I let her have her way for six months but kept giving her a little bit more as time went on. In reality, I was using the "aim small, miss small" principle from chapter 1. I gave her small things to do, and as she grew, I gave her more. She didn't even know what I was doing, but her self-esteem began to grow.

We kept working together, then after a while, I said, "Hey, I'm leading our mission trip to Mexico. You want to come with me?"

She said, "Cool. Yeah, I'll go."

She came the first year as my assistant. The second year, I said, "How about we lead together?" So, we split the ministry. The third year, I said, "How about you lead it? I'll serve you now." By the fourth year, I told her I wasn't going; she was now leading the trip. Now, she leads mission trips all over the world. Step by incremental step is a valuable investment.

Investment requires time, but with patience and persistence, it works. Investment is giving of your time, effort, and what you know. Investment requires a lot of you to walk deep in people's messes and see their diamonds, pull them out, and polish them. It is hard work but the fruit of that kind of investment is priceless.

A Caring Investment: One of the churches I worked at had a boys' program. The gentleman serving in ministry there was the only leader who was working at the time. This guy was roughshod, and although he had a great heart and a faithful, teachable spirit, he did not have a thorough understanding of what leadership was supposed to be like.

I said, "You're gonna serve with me. You're gonna walk with me."

And he said, "Yes, ma'am."

He walked with me for a year and then ran that program effectively for many years after. It was the most successful boys' program in our state. There's an investment, but it took time and caring about him as a person, not just as someone who serves.

Churches are filled with stories of leaders using someone to serve but not caring about what they're walking through. That's called abuse, and the church must stop doing that. People matter, and we must care about what they're going through, not just what they can do for us and the ministry. We have to care about them, we have to walk with them in their mess, and we have to care about where they're walking. When people know you're investing in them in a caring way, it's a whole different level, and you begin to rise personally as a leader, and you begin to make them rise.

However, we are always to remember we're not Jesus. We're not here to carry their sins; we're not here to make them dependent on us. That's a mistake. And sometimes out of the kindness of our hearts, we step in too far. There's a line. Our job is to point others to Christ not ourselves.

Faithful Investment: On my third mission trip to Mexico, we had VBS in the middle of an open field called the Colli, the poorest part of the city of Guadalajara. It's so poor the children put on their best clothes because for them VBS is their Disneyland. Their clothes are ripped, their shoes are ripped, but it's the best they have. And they've worn their best for the gringos who have come.

When we arrived, the missionary told us to prepare for 220 kids. I suggested we plan for 300, and she agreed. We prepared snacks and supplies for 300 because we're doing VBS for four days.

We learned that these kids are so poor that the mommies feed their daughters on one day and feed the sons on the next day because they don't have enough food. But the children share the food. So the boys will come with their sandwiches and give half to their sisters, and the girls will share with their brothers the next day. So when I bring a snack, I don't bring a bag of chips; I bring a whole box of cereal per kid.

On the third day, the attendance hit 300, and I was super excited.

A Buddhist woman who helped us said, "I'll help you with whatever you're doing for the children." (Buddhists look at this as a humanitarian effort.) So right before we distributed snacks on the fourth day, she said, "Pastor, you got a really big problem. We have 300 snacks and over 400 children. I've counted them seven times."

I was shocked. Now what? There's no Costco. We're in the jungle. I said, "Team, come on. We have an issue." What's my job as a leader? To know the way, go the way, and show the way. I said, "Team, we're gonna pray over the snacks."

They all came running over, and the Buddhist woman asked, "What are you doing right now?"

I said, "We're gonna pray over the snacks."

She was confused.

I said, "Well, there's a story in the Bible about God feeding 5,000 people with five fishes and some loaves."

She said, "You think God will multiply the snack?"

And I said, "I'm going to ask Him to do it."

She was furious with me. She stormed over to the missionary and told her what we were doing.

The missionary said, "That's a great idea," and joined us.

So the team and I prayed over the snacks, and when snack time came, I said, "Are you ready to give out snacks?"

We set the kids down and started walking around with boxes of juice and packages of crackers. We handed out 270, 280, 290, 300, 310, 320, 330, 340, 350, 360, 370, 380, 390, 400, 410, 420. We had more than enough snacks with one full box of snacks left over! You know who was holding the box? The Buddhist woman!

She was standing there, holding a full box. Tears were running down her face, and she asked, "What just happened? What just happened?"

I knew the way, I walked the way, and I led the way. And that was just the beginning of the many miracles we saw right before our eyes. My team went the following year without me and witnessed their own miracles!

That's how faithful investment works. As you pour in, as you invest, as you build people, they can begin to do the same thing. But I would be remiss not to mention the flip side of investment.

The Investment of Risk

It's a word that will always come when you talk about any type of investment, especially financial. It's the word, *risk*. And I would be remiss by not mentioning it because no one warned me about this when I came out of Bible school. You can invest, and you can pour your heart into people, but sometimes it doesn't work out the way you think it should. As a matter of fact, sometimes it backfires. And the people you've invested in now either hate you or hate the Lord. That's something we don't talk about, but we need to because this is where leaders lose it.

How is it that I have poured into this person, and now I'm the bad guy? I've invested in this person; now I'm terrible? How did that happen? I was up in the middle of the night praying with them; I brought them food; I've walked with their family; I've prayed for them, and now I'm the monster? Or she doesn't want to serve the Lord? Or she has turned away?

Can I tell you that sometimes those broken people just stay broken, and sometimes they try to break other things because that's what they know. It's not because they're evil. It's because they're hurt, or they're broken. And that is something you have to understand. Investment comes with a component of risk. It has to. Or it's not a real investment.

You can't really invest money unless there's a risk you could lose it. That's the thing—you can't truly invest in people without the possibility of them turning away. Think about even Jesus. He invested in the Twelve, but even one of His betrayed Him. We're no better than him. We're going to invest in people who aren't always going to work out. Can I tell you something? Invest anyway. Pour anyway. Give anyway. Because you're not doing it for them, and I learned that a long time ago. There are plenty of people out here investing like, "I don't even like this person, but I've given everything I have. They don't listen; they don't learn." My job is to invest in the person I believe God has called them to be, not the person you actually see. You invest and you pour into people because you are doing it unto the Lord. You see who God wants to make them not who they currently are.

I heard a story that rocked me to my core, and I want to share it with you. It is heart breaking, but it will greatly help us understand how leaders who are willing to get dirty can change someone's life.

When Leaders Get Dirty

Years ago, a fourteen-year-old girl was removed from her home and her parents and placed in a Christian foster home. The person in charge of the home was a great leader. They had very little information on this girl, but they knew her father was beating her. She came to the house, and the first night she seemed fine. She was shown her room, she unpacked, and got ready for bed. When they went to wake her up in the morning, her room smelled terrible. They found feces smeared all over the walls.

The foster staff got the director who quickly told everyone not to ask the girl why she did this. She went to the girl and gently asked, "Would you help me clean this?"

The girl said yes, so they cleaned together, no questions asked. The second morning came, and there were feces all over the wall again. The director did exactly the same thing. This went on for weeks, and each day, the girl and the director cleaned the wall together.

Finally, the director said, "You can tell me why you are doing this. You won't get into any trouble."

The girl felt safe with the director because of all the weeks of helping clean her mess, so she told her story. Her father had been raping her for years, and one time as he was raping her, she became so upset she defecated on herself. He was so disgusted that he left. After that, every time he tried to rape her, she would defecate, and he would leave her alone. Finally, she started smearing it on the walls before he came in. And he never tried again, although he beat her for smearing the walls, but she did not stop doing it. So for her, the smell of feces meant safety.

The director told her that she could do that for as long as she needed until she felt safe. She continued for a few more weeks, then she began only smearing one wall, and then finally she stopped altogether.

That director walked with her every step of the way. The girl is an adult now, healed and walking in victory—all because one leader was willing to get dirty. Literally.

That leader taught this girl that Jesus was her source of safety. The director walked with the girl in her mess until God had healed her. This is our job: to meet people where they are and walk with them. It will be messy and dirty, and it will cost us something, but that is the life of true leadership.

Application for Leaders

It's our responsibility to invest in others, to invest in the people closest to us in the ministry. People walk through life with a wide range of circumstances and situations, and we must invest, speak life, encourage, and even get dirty with them, no matter what happens.

Sometimes we must be silent in our leadership, and other times we must speak out. As you begin to speak life into someone, you're not necessarily talking to that person, but you're pulling out from them what God has put into them. Walk with God and don't get in the flesh. As you walk beside them, with God in focus, you will see them grow, see them stretch, see them begin to expand their own spheres of influence. And even if you don't get to, that doesn't mean you stop investing.

Consider who has invested in you, bringing you to where you are now. How much influence did that leader have in your life? Because they walked with you, they invested in you, they called life out of you, they loved and cared for you. And now here you sit, being able to reproduce the same leadership in someone else's life.

Strive to be a level 4 leader. Strive not to build systems or programs, but strive to build people, understanding that there is always a risk involved. But even with the risk, there's great reward because there is always a diamond in the rough. And the way to pull the diamond out of people is to begin to see something remarkable in them that they themselves don't see. Begin to speak hope and faith in ways they can't see. And soon, the reward will be fantastic because when you see someone begin to walk in what God has for them, there is no greater feeling. Invest much in others as a leader, and let God do the rest!

CHAPTER SEVEN

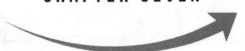

Living between "Hosanna" and "Give Us Barabbas"

OUT OF ALL THE chapters in this book, this chapter is by far the most personal because I have learned its contents in the battle and seasons of ministry. I've learned this concept in my many years serving, first as a child growing up in ministry, then in Bible school, and then serving in eight different churches, including my childhood church, an ethnic church, a storefront church, a deaf church, and a mega church. These are lessons I've learned that I've tried to teach every young minister I work with because I believe that they are truly the downfall of many leaders. The downfall is not understanding how to live between "Hosanna" and "Give Us Barabbas."

THE COURAGE TO LEAD

Jesus and His Experience with "Hosanna" and "Give Us Barabbas"

I want to break down this concept with a biblical illustration. John 12 starts with what we call Palm Sunday. Jesus was riding through town on a donkey, and the people recognized Him as the Messiah. They became so elated that they laid palm branches on the ground. They worshiped Him saying, "Hosanna, Hosanna. Glory to God. Hosanna." By definition *hosanna* is the highest form of praise. They waved their palm branches and were filled with joy because to them, Jesus was the most radiant, beautiful person they had ever seen.

Jesus rode through the town, receiving their praise and worship. Then He began to teach all those people gathered. They listened, and then He went with His disciples to have the Last Supper. Jesus ate with His disciples, and He predicted His own demise at this supper. The disciples were perplexed because they just saw how the people worshiped him. He even told Peter, one of His key disciples, that Peter himself was going to deny Him three times.

Then He said that one of them would betray Him. He is talking about Judas, although He doesn't say his name.

The Lord told them what is to come, and the disciples were baffled because what they had just seen didn't match what He said was going to happen. Soon, Jesus was sold out by Judas like a piece of property, arrested by a mob of soldiers, and betrayed by those who were closest to Him. Yet one of the most profound moments was when Jesus was brought to trial. A crowd had gathered, and Pontius Pilate asked them, "What should I do with Jesus? What would you like me to do with Him now that He's been arrested, now that He has these charges brought against Him?"

These people yelled, "Crucify Him! Crucify Him! Crucify Him!"

Pilate asked, "But what has He done? What has He done that you want Him to be crucified?"

The Bible says they couldn't answer the question. They just yelled louder, "Crucify Him! Crucify Him! Crucify Him!" They didn't even know why they wanted Him crucified. Then the governor said it was the practice during this season that they would release a criminal, and he asked, "Who would you want me to release, Jesus or Barabbas?" thinking that if they had a true criminal in front of them, they'd release Jesus and crucify the criminal.

They said, "Give us Barabbas. Crucify Jesus!"

The governor was shocked and didn't understand. He continued to ask the people whom they wanted released, and each time they yelled, "Give us Barabbas, and crucify Jesus!"

So Pilate gave them exactly what they wanted, and Jesus was crucified. (John 19: 4–16, author's paraphrase.)

We're so grateful for the second part of the story, though, because Jesus doesn't stay dead and was resurrected three days later. But I want to take something from this biblical account and apply it to the realm of today's leadership.

The same people yelling, "Give us Barabbas and crucify Jesus" are the same people who, only a few days prior, were yelling, "Hosanna!" and laying palm branches down at Jesus's feet and worshiping Him. These are the same people who have gone from worshiping Jesus to demanding His demise!

The Nature of Man

If Jesus had not had any real contact with these people, what in the world would cause them to go from "Hosanna" to "Give us Barabbas" in just days? I'm going to tell you what it is. It is the nature of man. The nature of man is fickle, the nature of man is self-serving, and the nature of man is selfish. The nature of man will always seek what the popular majority or the group wants. And because these people are easily swayed and easily moved, the Bible compares them to sheep. Sheep are easily tricked and easily moved around. So, these people have changed; their fickle hearts have flipped from honoring Jesus to wanting to have Him killed. Such an unbelievable turn of events.

It is sad to say that there is really no difference today when we deal with people and leadership. This biblical illustration paints a powerful and painful picture for every leader. You can live in the praise of men, which I call the "Hosannas," or you can live in the criticism of men, which I call the "Give us Barabbas." Or you can simply walk the straight path and live for neither, serve neither, and simply lead to please the Lord.

The Difference between "Hosannas" and "Give Us Barabbas"

It's easy for a leader in any capacity to become utterly discouraged due to the seemingly polar opposites you experience from time to time. One day you are the greatest, kindest, gentlest, most amazing leader. You have been there for them, you have cared for them, and you've been faithful to them. Those are the "Hosanna" times.

The next day, people are angry with you, and they hate you. They have nothing good to say about you, or they ignore you, and you don't know why. This is the "Give Us Barabbas" times. These are the same actions Jesus dealt with in biblical times: the fickleness and selfishness of men. Today's leaders deal with the same thing.

When People Have Expectations

We bump into this thing that causes man to go from "Hosanna" to "Give Us Barabbas" when we can't meet their expectations. We simply can't make every person happy; we are critiqued, given demands, and are looked upon as bad or uncaring leaders because we don't meet their expectations. What is expected of a leader is often unrealistic and sometimes ungodly.

Many leaders I know personally have walked away from the ministry because of unrealistic expectations. Many leaders have walked away from or have been destroyed by the ministry because they can't manage the tension these expectations create. They don't understand it, and it's heartbreaking for them.

But leaving the ministry doesn't have to be your response. We can definitely learn from Jesus's example. It doesn't have to be something that destroys you. It can be something you grow from because I truly believe the leadership that's going to survive, blossom, and move forward is the leadership that understands how to live in the tension of both praise and criticism. Neither is the right place to live, and you can't allow either to define or motivate you or your ministry.

Living in the "Hosanna"

It is easy to get caught up in the "Hosanna" because when we walk with people and pour our lives into them, we are good leaders. If we preach a good message or we sing a good song, it feels good to our flesh to receive praise. It's not a bad thing for people to say, "You did a good job," "Thank you so much," or "I appreciate what you've done." The problem for leaders comes when we begin to look for these things, when we begin to look for these accolades that bless us, make us feel good, or make us feel accomplished. If we begin to do that, we've moved into living in the "Hosanna," and that's a dangerous place to be. Let me share an example of what this looks like.

Years ago, I worked for a senior pastor who was a great preacher and because of that, he was invited to preach in several countries oversees. One Sunday morning after he had returned from preaching in London, I noticed something different about him as he was preaching. He kept referring to all the things that *he* had accomplished oversees, the people *he* had blessed, the people *he* had healed. Then he said that we, as a church, were fortunate to have him as our pastor. My heart dropped because he was believing all the praise he was receiving. He now thought he was the gift instead of the servant.

Things got worse, and no one could say anything to him. He only wanted people around him who said "Yes, Pastor." No other opinion was welcomed because he was always right. Finally, more than half the church left. However, he still did not see what was happening, and soon he lost it all, including everyone and his ministry. All because he lived in the "Hosannas."

Living in the "Hosannas" can also mean that I don't feel like I'm doing a good job unless someone is praising me. I look for others to affirm my ministry or leadership. I need or desire their praise to feel accomplished. And if I don't receive it, I don't feel like I'm doing well. Now the "Hosannas" become my reward and ultimately my demise.

Living in the "Give Us Barabbas"

Not only is it hard to live in the "Hosannas," it is equally hard to live in the "Give Us Barabbas" times. Mankind will never be satisfied because we are not called to please and serve man—we are called to please and serve God. As I have said, this chapter is very personal for me. In my years of ministry, I have worked in many churches, and each time God has used me as a trailblazer. I have walked into very sick churches with broken people, broken systems, and poor leadership. Yet each time, God has asked me to lead and to lead strong. That has always come with a company of critics. I have been yelled at, cursed at, mistreated, underpaid, criticized, and even threatened.

One specific time in the ministry, I poured my life into this couple who were in crisis. I was there for them and walked with them daily. I prayed, counseled, supported, and cried with them. I made myself available the best way I knew how. They always said how thankful they were for my support and help. Their words were, "We don't know where we would be without you."

One day during this eight-month ordeal, I could not meet with them. They lost their minds because I did not drop everything for them on that day. They verbally attacked me, they bad mouthed me to the church, and they went to the senior pastor and tried to get me fired. All because I did not meet their unrealistic expectation. Thankfully, the pastor knew the truth, but I was hurt and truly confused. I was young in the ministry, and this threw me for a loop and really broke my heart for a season. I learned quickly that as a leader, I must be secure in my calling because it will be challenged by people who have unrealistic expectations that I cannot meet. If you want to be an effective leader, you will be criticized and mistreated. Effective leaders have to make strong decisions, and often it will not make everyone happy. You can't let that stop you from doing what you have to do as a leader. You will never be effective if you fear the backlash of man.

Living in the Middle

I could fill this book with story after story of instances of praise and instances of criticism, but what is most important here is that we can't worry about pleasing the people we serve. Charles Spurgeon said it like this, "What has cured me of the fear of men is the fear of God." In other words, our life must please Jesus and Jesus only.

We cannot live in the "Hosannas" because "Hosannas" have to do with what we have done, and we have done nothing. We don't work for people; we work for the Lord. Therefore, my praise, my thanks, and my reward should never come from people. It should always come from the Lord. That doesn't mean people can't be polite or that they can't be grateful. It doesn't mean that they can't bless me, but I can't expect them to do it or let that be my reward.

First of all, we must realize something about our identity. We can't find it nor look for it in the praise of others. The Lord Himself will bless us. He will take care of us. He will guard our lives. We have to allow Him to give us these things, so we need to keep looking toward Jesus and not toward the "Hosannas." It's true; people are welcoming. People can be very gracious. People can be very thankful for what you've done for them, or they could admire you for the anointing on your life, and that's okay. But we must not live in it.

We cannot live in the praise; we cannot believe our own hype. Another way of saying that is we cannot buy our own press. We are servants; we are never to be praised. We must never think we are a gift to people. Jesus is the gift, and we are simply His servants. We must realize that we are not the gift to all, but the servant of all. We must be aware of who we are— frail humans serving frail humans. If we recognize our weaknesses and failures, realizing that we are nothing but dust and our only strength comes from the anointing of the Lord Jesus Christ, then we will truly know who we are, and we will be able to live in that tension. I'm so grateful that God uses me, but in Scripture, God has always used imperfect vessels, and often we are no better than that. We are just a tool He uses.

We can't live in the "Give Us Barabbas" either. As a true leader, I must honor God first. I can't let man stop me from leading and leading strong. If you are truly doing the will of God, you will have critics, but you have to keep leading. People can be cruel and ungodly when they don't get their way. They may hurt your feelings and say and do awful things; forgive and move on. Don't sit there; do the will of God with grace and courage. That is the only way you can have longevity and effectiveness in your leadership.

Courageous leader, you must learn how to live right smack down the middle between "Hosannas" and "Give Us Barabbas"—right in the tension of both. How does this work? Let God thank you and praise you. Let Him be the one who humbles you because He knows how to keep you in check. That is what walking in the middle of both praise and criticism means.

Application for Leaders

We love the praise of others and hate the criticism of others. Colossians tells us to live a life fully pleasing the Lord and not human beings. So that's always the challenge when living between these extremes. Our only talent is what He has given us, and the only platform that's been open to us is one to which He has elevated us.

As we remove our identity from the praise of others and toward the Lord, He will bless us and take care of us. He will guard our lives, but we can't look for these things. As we allow the Lord to give us things that empower us as leaders, we can walk, not seeking the "Hosannas," but understanding and appreciating people's gratitude. Soon we begin to see a big difference in the anointing on our lives because anything in the ministry is from God and God alone. Even the criticism of others will be deflected because we realize our own failings and humanity and recognize that God works through us to ensure that we lead according to His will and His Word.

God loves us, cares for us, and has placed us in the ministry in which we serve. Therefore, He will reward us. If we keep in mind that the "Hosannas" are nice, but they are not life giving. The criticism is not desirable, but it helps us self-reflect and keeps us focused on God. We must maintain that right perspective that our boss is the Lord Jesus Christ. That's who we work for, and that's who we long to please.

CHAPTER EIGHT

The Key Ingredient to Leadership Is Faithfulness

WHEN WE LOOK AT leadership, there is a key ingredient we must possess to be truly effective: faithfulness. As a leader facing many demands and responsibilities, it's hard to maintain that fine line of faithfulness. Sometimes it is not even demands or responsibilities; it is simply being weary. Yet we are called to be leaders, and we are called to serve and build up people even when it is difficult or seemingly without fruit. True results take years. It never comes overnight or quickly. Faithfulness is the key to great leadership and lasting fruit.

As we explore this idea of faithfulness, there are three elements to help establish faithfulness in your leadership and in your life. The first element of faithfulness is choice. We choose to be faithful. Though it sounds simplistic, I believe many decisions start with an act of the will. The psalmist is constantly making the decision to be faithful to God as he says, "I will bless the Lord." So much more should we choose to be faithful to God.

The second element of faithfulness is to plant. We should let our lives be planted in faithfulness. What does that look like? Faithfulness is part of the fruit of the Spirit, and we cannot grow in the fruit of the Spirit if we have not planted the seed of the Word in our lives. The Word of God is what causes the things of God to grow in us.

The third element is action. If we want to be an incredible, effective, and anointed leader, we must lead with action. This involves being loyal in our relationship with the Lord. We must be diligent in serving the Lord. As we spend time with God in prayer and in the Word, we learn how to live His Word. You may say, "I already know this!" But knowing and doing are two different things. We can dream all day, but unless we put some action behind that desire, it's simply that: a desire. Leaders fall into the same traps as everyone else, so we must be vigilant toward action.

To even begin to be a faithful leader, we must take account of our lives and look at the areas we're truly not faithful in. Be honest. Ask yourself, "Am I diligent? Am I trustworthy? Am I loyal? Do I persevere?" Look at it with the mirror of the Holy Spirit as you evaluate your relationships with people, your jobs, your marriages, and your ministries. If each leader would allow the Holy Spirit to examine their faithfulness, they would truly understand that the only way fruit grows is with diligent care and the seed of the Word.

Four Seeds of Faithfulness

Faithfulness is made up of four components: loyalty, diligence, trust, and perseverance. All four components are like seeds that when combined together, give us the fruit of faithfulness. God is looking for leaders who, when He gives something or someone to them, exemplify these four things. Often, many leaders tell me about what they want from God. They want a powerhouse relationship with the Lord; they want to be champions in the Kingdom, but I ask them about their faithfulness, and I often find it lacking.

If the seeds of faithfulness are to produce the fruit of faithfulness, then why is it lacking? We must go back to the three elements of faithfulness: choosing, planting, and taking action. But most often, we don't get past the first element: choice. Leaders don't want to put in the work. That is understandable because leadership is hard, dedicated work, but that's because you're only looking at one component of faithfulness. What about the other seeds of faithfulness: loyalty, diligence, trust, and perseverance? Are you always diligent? Do you invest in your marriage and in others? Are you loyal with your words and with your actions? Do you persevere when there's trouble, or do you throw up your hands and give up? God desires for us to say, "I will be faithful in all four of these pieces. I will be loyal. I will be diligent. I will be trustworthy. I will persevere. I choose to be faithful."

See, faithfulness has many components, and if we look at it one dimensionally, we look pretty good. But if we look at it fully, each one of us has some work to do. You see, leaders, we live in a world that rewards talent and gifting. Look at award shows like *MTV* or the *Golden Globes*. Look at the people who are honored and why they're honored. They're talented. They're gifted. They look good, but God's economy is different.

God does not reward the talented—He rewards the faithful. He rewards those who endure. The Bible is clear that the race is not given to the swift nor the battle to the strong. It's given to him who endures forever. God's economy rewards faithfulness, not talent or gifting. When we get to Heaven, He's not going to ask you what type of car you drove or what your credit score was. He could care less about your degree, so He is not going to ask about that. He is going to ask, "Have you been faithful with everything I've given you? Have you been faithful with everything I've put before you, big or small?" He is not going to say, "Well done, thou good and *successful* servant." He's going to say, "Well done, good and *faithful* servant" (Matt. 25:23 author emphasis).

God's not interested in how the world markets success. He's interested in how faithful we are with what we've been given. We lead with faithfulness and serve others for His glory, and only for His glory. For the sake of illustration, let's look at the greatest example of faithfulness in the Bible: the story of Ruth.

Naomi and Ruth: Examples of Faithfulness

The key ingredient of faithfulness in leadership is found in Ruth 2. Naomi and her husband lived in Judah when a massive famine hit the land, forcing them to uproot with their two sons, and go to Moab, a pagan place. Those people worshiped idols, yet Naomi and her family had no choice. They had to survive. While there, Naomi's husband died, and she was left with her two sons. Then her two sons married two Moabite women, and the five of them lived together for about ten years when both of Naomi's sons also died. Then Naomi was left with her two daughters-in-law.

She again had to figure out how to survive. Naomi decided that the best thing to do was to go back to Judah. She's heard that the famine has lifted, and she wanted to go back to her people and try and make a life for herself. The first thing she did was to release her daughters-in-law. She said, "Go. Go back to your people. Go back to your families. Go get new husbands. Go get a different life," but both girls clung to Naomi saying, "We won't leave you."

Then Naomi insisted, "Look, I'm old. I'm not going to have more sons. I don't have anything to give you. Go back to your families. There is no future with me" (Ruth 1:8–12, author's paraphrase).

Orpah leaves, but the other, Ruth, refused to leave. She grabbed her mother-in-law, she cried over her, and she clung to her. She made a pledge to her mother-in-law saying, "Entreat me not to leave you or to turn back from following after you; for wherever you go, I will go; and wherever you lounge, I will lounge; your people shall be my people, and your God, my God. Where you die, I will die, and there will I be buried. The Lord do so to me, and more also if anything but death parts you and me" (Ruth 1:16–17).

An incredible pledge. It's a hard argument to fight. So, Naomi and Ruth went back to Judah. They ended up in Bethlehem, and then had to figure out how to survive once again. There was some land left by Naomi's husband, and though it hadn't been taken care of in years, Naomi and Ruth settled there. They tried to rebuild their land. Ruth took on the role of trying to provide for herself and her mother-in-law.

There was a practice in those days called *gleaning* where the women, mostly poor women, would go behind the reapers after the harvest and gather leftover barley and grain. The women gathered this food for their families, but it was a dangerous practice. Women were often assaulted and abused in these fields by the men who were there. Most of the time, the women tried to glean together in clusters, but you have to realize something. Ruth was a pagan and a foreigner, and the people of Judah did not welcome her with a celebration party. They welcomed her with gossip. But even so, Ruth set out to glean alone in order to provide for her family. In Ruth, chapter 2, we see a switch.

We are introduced to a gentleman by the name of the Boaz. Boaz was Naomi's relative. He owned a lot of land and was a man of great wealth. When Naomi told this to Ruth, Ruth asked if she could go glean grain from Boaz's field so that she might find favor in his sight. Naomi sent Ruth out with her blessing. And we find a wonderful first encounter between Ruth and Boaz in Ruth 2:4–12.

> Now behold, Boaz came from Bethlehem and said to the reapers, "The Lord be with you," and they answered him, "The Lord bless you." Then Boaz said to his servant who was in charge of the reapers, "Who's young woman is this?" So the servant, who was in charge of the reapers answered and said, "It is the young Moabite who came back with Naomi from the country of Moab. And she said, 'Please let me glean and gather after the reapers among the shearers.'

So she came and has continued from morning until now, though she rested a little in the house."

Then Boaz said to Ruth, "You will listen, my daughter, will you not? Do not glean in any other field, nor go from here, but stay close to my young women. Let your eyes be on the field which they reap, and go after them. Have I not commanded my young men not to touch you? And when you are thirsty, go to the vessels and drink from what the men have drawn."

So she fell on her face, bowed down low to the ground, and said to him, "Why have I found favor in your eyes, that you shall take notice of me, since I am a foreigner?" Boaz answered to her and said, "It has been fully reported to me, all that you have done for your mother-in-law since the death of your husband, and how you have left your father and your mother and the land of your birth, and have come to a people who you did not know before. The Lord repay your work, and a full reward be given to you by the Lord God of Israel under whose wings you have come for refuge."

Boaz heard about all that Ruth had done, and as the story unfolds, Boaz was given the opportunity to redeem the land of Naomi's husband. In doing so, he was given the opportunity to marry Ruth, and he does! In one moment, God repaid Ruth all she had given. In one sweeping moment, God handed her back everything she had given up. Everything.

If we follow the story, Boaz and Ruth give birth to Obed, who happened to be the father of Jesse, who happened to be the father of David, who is in the lineage of our Lord and Savior

Jesus Christ. Talk about redemption! Ruth, a faithful Moabite, is the great, great, great grandmother of Jesus!

I am not a believer in coincidence or chance. I don't believe things just happen. I believe God is divine, and He is constantly at work in the lives of His people. Whether we see it, or whether we know it, God is at work. I believe that as Ruth was faithfully gleaning the fields, the Holy Spirit inched her toward the fields of Boaz and put her right in his sight.

Scripture says that Ruth and Naomi happened to arrive in Bethlehem during harvest time. They might have thought that they just happened to arrive, but it was the Holy Spirit saying to Naomi, "It's time to go back home." She didn't know it, she didn't feel it, she didn't understand it because she was grieving the death of her family, yet God was still at work in her life. God was still moving in her life, and He inched her over to where He needed her to be, the same way He inched Ruth over to where they both needed to be for His glory.

Faithfulness in the Modern-Day Leader

Leaders, like in the story of Ruth, Naomi, and Boaz, God is constantly at work in our lives, whether or not we see it, know it, or understand it. God is diligent in getting us into His divine will and His divine plan because there is a divine will and a divine plan for each one of His children. We know that His plan is good, but I believe there was something in Ruth's DNA and in her character that gave God access to move in her life. Her faithfulness was a key ingredient and is the same key ingredient in our lives that will allow us to walk in God's divine will. Faithfulness is also the key ingredient found in great and lasting leadership.

In everything she did, Ruth was faithful. She did everything with all her heart and with everything that was in her. Even a job as dirty as gleaning in the field, Ruth did with all her might. She was doing it with all her being. It was her faithfulness that won Boaz's heart.

It might have been her appearance that caught his eye. She was probably beautiful, but what got his heart was her testimony. He said, "I have heard of all that you've done" (Ruth 2:11, author's paraphrase). Basically, he was saying, "I've heard of your faithfulness to your mother-in-law. I've heard of how you've given up everything and clung to her, how you vowed to take care of her, and you have." It was Ruth's faithfulness that won Boaz's heart.

God is always looking for faithful leaders, and He found one in Ruth. Because of that, He was able to bless her. Likewise, God is looking for faithful leaders today. God is looking for people to whom He can entrust things, and whatever He gives them, they will do with all their hearts, whether big or small. God's looking for leaders who are faithful, who don't quit when it gets hard, and who will always work as unto the Lord and not unto man.

Faithful in the Small Things

Let me illustrate this idea of being faithful in the small things with my own experience. When I graduated from Bible school, all my friends had big positions. I had been offered positions, and God said no to all of them. I don't know what it is like in secular college, but when you graduate from Bible college, everyone wants to know what you're going to do.

"Oh, I'm going to Massachusetts."

"I'm going here."

"I'm going there."

"Where are you going?" people would ask me.

"I'm going home," I replied. "I'm going home. God closed all the doors."

So I went home, back to my home church. There was a new pastor who did not believe in women leading in ministry. He called me into his office for an interview and said, "Listen. I don't want to, but everyone's breathing down my neck to hire you because you're a daughter of this church. This is how it's going to work. I'll offer you the Assistant Superintendent of the Children's Department position. There's going to be a man over you. He doesn't even have to come in, but his title will go before yours. You can do all the work but will not have the title—the guy will have it. That is the offer I am giving you. What do you say?" (By the way, there was no salary either.)

I wanted to answer in my flesh, but the Lord told me to take it, so I told the pastor I would. He was shocked. He wasn't the only one who was shocked. I was too. Why in the world would God ask me to take this position? I worked there for two years, and I did all the work, never once meeting the guy who was in charge.

One day as I was sweeping the bathroom in the children's gym, I had a real moment with God. I said, "God, I've had prophesies over my life since I was a baby about how You were going to use me and the things that You wanted from me. I've been to Bible school. I graduated. I have such a heart to do things for You, and this is it? This is it, God? I'm going to sweep a bathroom for the rest of my life?"

I was waiting for God to comfort me or reassure me, but He did not. He said something so profound that it changed my life and my understanding of leadership. God said very plainly, "And so what if it is?"

I froze, and at that moment, I realized what He was saying. Would I be faithful no matter the task, big or small? If this little task would bring Him glory, would I be faithful to Him and the ministry for the rest of my life?

I said, "To You be the glory, God. I'll do it. I will sweep this floor with all my heart and with all my might. If that's what's going to bring You glory, You are going to find me faithful."

I worked in that church for the next couple of months, and it just so happened that after that, I met a minister who needed a youth and children's pastor. It just so happened, but really it didn't just happen. God was looking for servant-leaders He could trust. When He can trust you, He'll give you more. That's the economy of God. Faithful in little, master over much. Are you faithful in a little? He will give you more. He wants to be able to give us more, but if He can't find us faithful in the small things, He will not be able to bless in the big things.

Faithful in the Big Things

On one of my mission trips to Guadalajara, we saw the team's faithfulness pay off right away! After an incredible VBS with 170 unsaved, unchurched kids showing up off the streets of Guadalajara, God literally gave us complete instructions, and my team was faithful in all that they did in this huge undertaking, no matter if it was big or small.

This group of kids gave their lives to the Lord by the end of VBS. After VBS, the pastor of that town showed up with all her teen-aged kids. We gave them our VBS T-shirts as a gift. She said, "This is my staff now. They're going to do VBS in the streets with me from now on." And they're doing it to this day.

We just faithfully obeyed the Lord in whatever He gave us. Whether we were sitting with the orphans or doing little Cheerio arts and crafts. Whatever it was, the team was simply faithful. I want to tell you that faithfulness opens the door for the supernatural! Let me tell you how this trip ended.

We arrived at the airport to fly back, and as is my practice, I intended on checking in last, but for some reason, this time I ended up checking in first. As I checked in, the woman at the ticket counter diligently looked at her computer, looked up at me, then looked down, typing away.

I asked, "Is there a problem?"

She said, "No, no," and she continued typing away.

I said, "There's a problem," and I grabbed the missionary because I don't speak Spanish. I said, "Ask her what the problem is."

The missionary told me that I wasn't on this flight.

I quickly handed the ticket agent the list of the whole team. I said, "Before they realize it, tell me who else is not on this flight?" There happened to be six of us who weren't on the flight.

The lady said, "Somehow in Newark, your tickets got messed up, and some of you were kicked off this flight."

I pulled the six who were not on the flight over to the side and explained what happened. Of course, everyone got emotional because now the team would have to be split up.

The Lord spoke to me clearly. He said, "Get rid of all your check-in baggage."

I turned to the team, the ten who were left. I said, "You guys have to take our check-in baggage."

They asked, "Why?"

I said, "The Lord said we've got to get rid of it."

They took it, and after they left, we went back to the ticket agent. Now six of us were left. We called ourselves the Sizzling Six because we believed God was going to spark something in us through this. We had nothing but our little carry-on bags, and the Lord said to me, "Tell your team to prepare to run." So, I did.

The ticket agent at the same moment looked up and said, "Can you guys run?"

I said, "Yes."

She said, "Please, please, please tell me you don't have any check-in bags."

I looked at her and said, "Not a one."

She said, "Last call. Let's go," grabbed the papers, and ran down the hall of Guadalajara airport. We were right behind her. She was able to go right up to the gate and get us on the next flight.

The faithfulness exhibited all week gave God a place, and we just happened to be there at the right time to receive the blessing.

Faithfulness Is Important to God

Do you know why faithfulness is so important to God? Because God is faithful. It is an attribute of God. He doesn't *possess* faithfulness. He *is* faithfulness. When we are faithful and we live lives that are loyal, diligent, trustworthy, and we persevere, we are now acting like Jesus!

I don't have a secular or earthly boss. My boss is the Lord Jesus Christ. I go to work each day, and I work for Him. Evangel was the first church I've ever worked in for a salary. I've worked in the secular world. I've had people sabotage my work because the favor of God is over my life. You know what I do? I work harder because I belong to Him. I'm only interested in His economy, not in man's economy.

Leaders, when tough things come against us, we're not supposed to run. We're supposed to persevere right through it. When it's hard, you've got to dig deep because that's when faithfulness shows up because it's the mark of a true leader. Everyone is faithful when things are easy, but true leaders show up when the cards are stacked against them. They stay loyal when everyone else doesn't. Loyalty is one of the greatest marks of godly leadership—loyalty to King Jesus and loyalty to one another. We must be married to loyalty and faithfulness, which is diligence in our vision, work, and mission. I don't just want to work well only when my boss is looking. I want to work well when he's not looking because I'm doing it as unto the Lord. When we are faithful and we live lives that are faithful, loyal, diligent, and trustworthy, and we persevere, and we allow these attributes to arise in us, we are now acting like Jesus. God uses situations in our lives to make faithfulness grow in us so He can make us more like Jesus.

Let me illustrate with a personal story of when I was traveling to Guadalajara with my mission team. I ask God to give a name to each team I lead; it gives a sense of identity and divine purpose. This team was the Highly Favored Fifteen and truly, that's who we were. We were on our fifth trip to Mexico with fifteen members. Five is the number of grace in the Bible, and grace was all over this trip. As we went down, I describe it this way: we got a kiss from Heaven in the beginning and an exclamation point at the end. We had to travel from New York to Houston, then Houston to Guadalajara. Not a big deal, except there's an hour layover. If you've ever traveled internationally, you know an hour layover is terrible, but as long as the plane leaves on time, we were good.

We got there, and the plane was on time. I got everybody on the plane then I picked up my phone to check the flight status. The flight is five minutes late, which is not a big deal, but then it's delayed ten minutes and finally twenty minutes. I tried to be calm because I'm in charge of the trip.

Then I heard the Lord simply say to me, "Am I faithful, or am I not faithful?"

I said, "Lord, you're faithful."

He said, "Put away your phone."

So, I put away the phone and told my team, "God is faithful, guys. We're going to be just fine." We are thirty-eight minutes delayed. All I was thinking is that the Houston airport is a bear. We have to land, find the gate, and I have to move all these people who don't know anything about international airports a long way to get to our flight, but the Lord said He was faithful.

We made our descent. I checked my phone to find the gate and started laughing. "Our next flight is delayed thirty-eight minutes." God gave us back every single minute! That was our little kiss at the beginning of our trip.

But our exclamation point came at the end of our trip. We had seen miracles. We saw God moving. We saw a VBS in the middle of one of the poorest neighborhoods in Guadalajara. Four hundred kids got to hear the gospel of Jesus Christ. They were saved. We saw children baptized in the Holy Spirit.

It was an unbelievable week, but we were exhausted at the end. On the way back, we have to go through Houston again. Now, the Houston airport has a weird philosophy if you're connecting from an international to a domestic flight. You have to pick up the bags you've checked in and re-check them. Not normally a big deal. But I have fourteen people with me. We have an hour and forty minutes, and it's our first entry back into the country, so we have to go through Immigrations, Customs, *and* checking our bags back in.

Usually, not a huge problem; however, we left twenty minutes delayed. I gave the team instructions on how we were going to do this. We zoomed through Immigrations. We zoomed through Customs. I split the team in half. Seven went to the gate. Eight came with me to get the bags. We got our bags and ran. We were booking it through Houston airport. Everything was going great, but then I realized John, one of my team members, was missing; TSA had flagged him. I said, "Everybody, go to the rest of the team. I'll wait for John."

I texted John to see what was going on. He said he had been flagged. We both started praying! A little later, I texted the team and said, "Pray. John got flagged."

They prayed. I texted John again: "John, how many people are waiting?"

He texted back, "There's six people in front of me."

"How many people are checking the bags?"

"One."

"How fast is he going?"

"Slow."

Each answer I didn't want to hear. I was like, "Okay. Can you tell them that our flight is leaving in twenty minutes?"

"I did. He said he doesn't care."

"Okay." I texted a team member on the other side of the airport. "Hey, tell the woman at the gate what's going on with us."

They texted back that the woman said she was sorry however we have fifteen minutes to make the flight.

I stood in the middle between two realities: what was happening and what I knew God can do. I just began to pray. I said, "Lord, you named this team the Highly Favored Fifteen. That's the name you gave us. Move on our behalf, God."

As I stood there, the chief of security walked by. I thought this must be the Lord. The Lord has brought him out. I went over and said, "Sir, can I talk to you?" I tell him our story.

He said, "Oh, I'm so sorry. You should go downstairs where your team member is so you can be with him when you both miss your flight." And then he walked away. I couldn't believe his answer!

Now I'm from Brooklyn, where we tend to get wound up easily. I had to take Brooklyn and calm it down for a minute. Then I realized that the voice I heard wasn't God's voice. It was the Enemy. It was a mocking voice.

At that moment I got righteously angry. I texted the team and said, "Hey, guys, this is warfare. Pray differently."

They were like, "We're on it."

I texted John: "John, is the line moving?"

"I'm number four."

"Okay." I texted the others: "Guys, what's going on?"

The team texted me: "We're loading on the plane." "We're all just praying." "We just told the flight attendant. She says she's so sorry, but you have seven minutes. Once they close the door, there's nothing they can do."

I texted back, "Okay." Then I got two texts at the same time. From the team: "They closed the door." From John: "I'm out."

I was about to have a stroke in the middle of the airport. I said, "Lord, what do I do?"

He said, "Go to the gate.

"Go to the gate? They closed the door."

"Go to the gate."

I texted John: "Meet me at gate 24," and then I ran across the Houston airport.

I got to the gate, and the marquee had changed to another plane. There was nobody there. I prayed, "Lord, what do you want me to do?"

He said, "Knock on the glass."

I started knocking on the glass.

Now everybody in the airport was watching this crazy person knock on the glass.

This man walked over and asked, "What are you doing?"

I think it's pretty obvious what I was doing. I said, "Sir, why are you asking?"

He said, "You should really just stop fighting. You missed your flight. Just go sit down."

In that moment I heard the same mocking voice. I said, "Sir, why don't you go sit down. This doesn't concern you."

He sat down, but with his arms folded, kind of just watching.

I kept knocking. I had no idea where John was. John could be in China for all I knew at this point. I continued to obey the Lord and kept knocking on the glass!

A man came out from behind the door. "Lady, what are you doing?"

"I'm trying to get on my flight." I said.

"That flight is gone. The door's shut," he said,

As he was telling me that, I heard the Lord say, "Tell Melinda to go talk to the captain."

I texted my lead team, "Melinda, go talk to the captain."

She texted, "Ah, the Holy Spirit just told me the same thing. I'm on it."

The teams kept me updated. Melinda ran to the front of the plane. She was talking to the flight attendant, who had opened the door for the captain to hear her. She talked to the captain. The team was praying. The whole plane was now waiting. The whole plane, according to the team, felt like electricity.

As this happened: John came running in. "Did we make our flight?"

I replied "We don't know yet."

He lifted up his hands in the middle of the waiting room and prayed, "God, I thank you that the heart of the king is in your hand, and You'll turn it anyway that You want, God."

The man who had talked to me from the desk said, "Listen, flight's over. Door's shut. The captain can't even open that door for a gunman. He would have to call the tower. They're not going to do it. This is not an emergency. You can sit there all day, make a tent, do whatever you want, you're not making your flight."

I said, "We're going to wait."

We were standing there praying. The people on the plane were praying. As the guy was getting ready for the next flight, the phone rang. He answered the phone. He put his head down then he looked up at me. He was in shock! His eyes start getting bigger and bigger.

My grin was getting bigger and bigger. I was just watching. I had my team on the phone. I said, "Melinda, they're going to open the plane."

"What?"

"They're going to open the plane."

I hung up and asked the ticket agent, "Sir, do you need me?"

He said, "Come over here. I need to issue you new tickets."

"Why is that?"

"Because apparently you know somebody who can open airline doors."

"Yes, I do. I know Jesus."

"That's the only person that could open this plane. That's it. It doesn't happen. Give me your tickets." He stamped our tickets.

John was still all pent up, but the ticket agent said, "Slow down. You don't have to worry about anything. You now are our VIP flyers. Houston airport has shut down for you two today." He escorted us to the door.

When we got on the plane, not just my team, the entire plane began to cheer and scream and clap. My team was on their feet going, "Jesus!"

And then the most beautiful thing happened. That flight home became a prayer meeting. People kept going, "Hey, since you guys know how to pray. Could you pray for . . ." All of a sudden, each team member had somebody they were ministering to on the flight home.

I sat there saying, "God, if this is not an exclamation point on this trip and Your faithfulness, I don't know what is."

That fifth Guadalajara mission trip was an amazing view of God's provision because of our faithfulness.

Application for Leaders

The rest of Ruth's life looked different because of her faithfulness. Ruth the Moabite ended up being in the lineage of Jesus. Jesus! Why? Because she was faithful. She wasn't gifted. She wasn't talented. She couldn't sell anything. She just knew how to be faithful, and God saw it. He said, "That's the marker I need to bless her," and He moved her right into His perfect will.

That is the same for you and me. Will you live lives that are faithful to the Lord? Will you exemplify faithfulness in all that you do—big, small, ministry related, or home related? Leaders, if you settle in your heart this pledge: "I am going to be faithful, loyal, trustworthy, diligent, I will persevere, and I am going to allow the fruit of the Spirit to grow in my life," I believe your whole life will look different.

The key to great leadership is faithfulness. Whatever's given to us, we must determine to accomplish it with all our hearts. Big or small, it doesn't matter. Leaders, we don't want things to just happen to us all day. We should want to walk in the will and the purpose of God because He alone makes His will happen. If our lives are found faithful, we have given God the tools to bless us. God now has an opportunity to move us into His divine plan.

As you continue to establish and grow faithfulness in your leadership and life, choose to be faithful, let your life be planted into faithfulness, and act purposefully in your relationship with the Lord, you will be effective leaders of faithfulness.

As people, and especially as leaders, we desire good things. And we can dream all day, but unless we put some action behind that desire, it's simply that. It's just the desire.

You must begin to take account of your life and look at the areas that you're not faithful in. Look at your marriages. Be honest. Am I diligent? Am I trustworthy? Am I loyal? Do I persevere? Look at it with the Holy Spirit mirror. Look at your relationships with people. Look at your jobs. Look at your ministries. I challenge every leader to allow the Holy Spirit to examine their faithfulness. And then we will truly understand that the only way fruit grows is with the seed of the Word!

CHAPTER NINE

Embracing the Beauty of the Process

THIS SEEMS TO BE an odd title especially as you go through the processes, the trials, and the struggles of leadership. Often we wouldn't categorize these processes as beautiful. However, I truly believe that our job is to embrace the processes we walk in and lead others through it as well. It's our job to grow personally and to show others how to begin to perceive the things that they walk through differently.

As leaders, we are meant to mature in the faith daily. We're meant to grow and to stretch. And often the process for growth is slow and painful. These are not words we like to hear because we like things that are quick and easy. The truth is, easier is not always better.

Would you rather eat a steak cooked in a microwave than on the grill? We might use the microwave out of necessity, but if we had our choice we'd fire up the grill any day of the week. But the grill requires a process. As we unpack the word *process,* we need to understand that things take time. And if you were to think of the tough things you're going through right now, you would not attach the word *beauty* to them.

You may challenge me by saying that the process is not beautiful. It's difficult. It's hard. It's strenuous. And all that is true. But I believe that Jesus is challenging us to see things a little differently. How you perceive things has a lot to do with how you walk through things. How you view things has a lot to do with how you process through them. Israel arrived at the Promised Land in eleven days. Five million people made it to the Promised Land in eleven days. They sent twelve spies into the land. All twelve came back and gave the same report.

Joshua said, "It is everything that God said. There's milk and honey. It's blessed. The fruit is unbelievable." Ten of them said, "But there are giants there. They're huge, and we can't take them. As a matter of fact, when we saw them, we felt like grasshoppers.'" And then the Bible says, "And so they became grasshoppers" (Num. 13, author's paraphrase). You see, their perception created something in them. How they perceived the giants and how they perceived themselves made them grasshoppers. They could have said they felt like lions in front of the giants, and the Bible would have said, "And so they became lions," but their faulty perception created their reality. Two of the spies said, "Yeah, there are giants there, but we can take them." But the two couldn't convince all of them. And so Israel wandered for the next forty years.

Perception means everything in how you view things, how you see things, and how you enter into things. Perception will determine whether you will grow or shrink. Either you will get stronger, or you will get weaker. Jesus made a blanket statement. He said, "In this world you will have trouble" (John 16:33 NIV). If you're not in trouble right now, you just came out of trouble, or you're about to be in trouble.

I'm so grateful for what Jesus says next: "But be of good cheer, I have overcome the world" (John 16:33). See, Jesus is creating a mindset for you. You're going to experience trouble, struggles, difficulties, and problems as a leader in the ministry. But be of good cheer, Jesus has overcome this world. And since Jesus has overcome it, He's given you the ability to overcome it. He didn't overcome simply for himself; He overcame it for us.

He has given you an arsenal of everything you need to overcome whatever comes your way. He's given you the grace. He's given you the power. He's given you the anointing. He's given you the Word. He's given you the Holy Spirit. Nothing is going to come into your life that can take you out. Except you.

Leader, I want you to learn this concept: Father filtered. Father filtered means that once you become a child of God, God is your Father, and there is a filter over your life. Nothing comes in your life that surprises God. He's not taken off guard by your struggle or by your hard times. He filtered it, and it doesn't really matter whether He brought it or He allowed it, He will use it. And this is where the beauty of the process comes in. Whether He brought it or whether He allowed it, He's going to use it in your life to make you into the image of Jesus. When you understand that, you begin to see the beauty in the process.

Then you begin to understand a little differently, and you lead differently. You will say, "Lord, this job is like working in hell. My co-workers are terrible. They treat me awfully. What are you trying to do with me, God?" If our perception was different. It might be terrible, but God is in control. He's allowing you to walk through it. What is He trying to produce and change in you? Is He trying to teach you to love people who don't act lovably? It's easy to love people who are nice to you. But we should love them when they're not nice. Love them when they sabotage you or want to hurt you. That's Jesus. That's not a better version of you; that's Jesus.

If you can grab hold of this, you can help your people immensely! You can lead like this: "I might not like it. It might be painful. It might be difficult. It might be heartbreaking, but in it we serve a God who can produce beauty from ashes. Ashes are nothing because they are things that have been destroyed. But out of that, God can produce beauty. God is not trying to make a better me, He's trying to make me like Him. And through the breaking and stretching and hard times, we embrace it because it is for our good." That is how you lead and lead strong.

Daniel, chapter 6, helps us with a picture of the beauty of the process.

The nation of Israel was captive in Babylon. The book of Daniel is considered a major prophecy because it spans the time of four kings. Everyone knows King Nebuchadnezzar, the most famous king in the book of Daniel. Actually, the king in chapter 6 was Darius. The people of Israel were slaves in Babylon. They had been there for many years. Darius said he wanted to establish governance and rulers, so he began to find the smartest and most accomplished men.

In the midst of all that came Daniel, this Jewish boy, and he stood out because he was an anointed Man of God. The favor and power of God was on him. He was a leader of leaders. He was wise, and he began to rise up. Daniel 6:3 says, "Then Daniel distinguished himself above the governors and satraps, because an excellent spirit was in him; and the king gave thought to setting him over the whole realm." And so there was Daniel, shining above all the Babylonians. The Bible says he had an excellent spirit. So the king said, "You know what, I might set him up over everything. I might make him the governor of all" (Dan. 6:3, author's paraphrase). Darius made Daniel the leader over all things.

The Babylonians were not happy with this Jewish slave being over them. They didn't recognize the favor of God. They began to set a plot in motion to trip him up. They searched through his life, and the Bible says they could find nothing. How powerful is that? So they decided to trip him up in his faith. They went to the king, and they spoke to the king's ego. They said, "Darius, we have an idea. We think that for the next thirty days, nobody should pray or talk to any other god but you. We think you should sign it as a decree, and if anybody defies it, they should be thrown in the lion's den" (Dan. 6:7, author's paraphrase).

Darius loved the idea, so he wrote the decree and signed it. And then the Bible says in verse 10, that Daniel heard about it: "Now when Daniel knew that the writing was signed, he went home. And in his upper room, with his windows open toward Jerusalem, he knelt down on his knees three times that day, and prayed and gave thanks before God as was his custom since early days." Despite what the decree said, Daniel couldn't pray to any other god but the one true God. And Daniel prayed to Him three times every day.

The men saw him, and they now had him breaking the law. They ran to the king and said, "Darius, Daniel has broken the law." Darius was upset because he loved Daniel. So he tried to procrastinate. He didn't do anything right away. He didn't do anything the next night, but the men kept pushing him. Finally, Darius said to Daniel, "I have to do this. But may the God that you serve continuously deliver you" (Dan. 6:16, author's paraphrase).

This ungodly king recognized the power of God's deliverance. The king threw Daniel into the lion's den. They put a huge rock over the den, and the king sealed it with his ring so no one could break it. They waited all night. The Bible says Darius didn't sleep, he didn't eat, and he had no music playing because he was lamenting. When the sun came up, Darius ran to the lion's den, moved the rock away, and yelled down, "Daniel, was your God able to save you?" (Dan. 6:20, author's paraphrase).

And Daniel said, "King Darius, live forever. King Darius, live forever. God sent angels to set the mouths of the lions. I am unharmed" (Dan. 6:22, author's paraphrase).

King Darius threw a party for God Jehovah—for Daniel's God. Darius gave honor. He gave homage. He gave worship to the God of Daniel.

Daniel was a slave, a prisoner in a foreign land. He was physically trapped, but the Bible said he had an excellent spirit. That means Daniel had his perception right. He knew that

God was in control of his life. He knew that God was faithful, and he was going to serve God whether he was in the stockade or whether he was walking free. He was going to have an excellent spirit because he didn't serve King Darius; he served God Almighty. He was going to lead the way God would have him lead. Daniel understood a principle that was much bigger than his current circumstance. And leader, you can go through hard stuff and have an excellent spirit because you can begin to understand it's not about this temporary thing you're walking through. There is a God over your life who is much bigger than the circumstance in front of you.

You can lead your people, and they will learn from you. You can get up well, you can go to work well, and you can live well. You can have an excellent spirit people will notice and say, "I know what she's going through, yet how does she have a smile on her face?" We have smiles on our faces because we know who owns us, we know who we belong to, and we know who's in control of our lives. And so we can walk through these temporary things—the struggles, the hard times—because they don't have to define us.

And for Daniel, being a prisoner in Babylon didn't stop him from being a son of Jehovah. It didn't define him. And through all that, he had an excellent spirit, and he walked before the Lord with excellence. I want to remind you of something: Daniel's life got harder because he did the right thing. God set him up because he did the right thing. He chose to lead in a godly, honoring way, and it all got harder. But what did he do? He continued to do the right thing. He continued to push forward in the right thing. He continued to honor God even when it got harder.

In this life, you will have trouble. And if you think Daniel had some supersonic power you and I don't have, then perhaps you are confused. Daniel was sent to the lion's den. He was the main character in one of the greatest accounts of a miracle in all of Scripture. We must remember that the resurrection hadn't happened yet. The power of the Holy Spirit hadn't come yet, so Daniel had what he had. But we have more because we have the power of the resurrection operating in our lives. The same power that raised Christ from the dead is at work today. We have the outpouring of the Holy Spirit. We have the whole book of the Bible, not half the book. While Daniel had the Holy Spirit come upon him, we have the Holy Spirit living in us. That's a big difference. We have the blood of Jesus and the anointing of the cross of Calvary. Daniel didn't have that yet. And still, he gave us one of the greatest accounts of leadership in Scripture.

How much more does God work in your life, leader? We have the same arsenal in front of us, ready to use. Like Daniel, we can embrace the process and lead through with our actions. And just as Daniel understood that what he was walking through was filtered by the Father, and God would grant him victory, we know that we serve the lion of the tribe of Judah who is over everything.

Leader, I want to put three ideas in your head to help you understand the beauty of the process. The first one is perception. Whatever you walk through, your victories and your defeats are going to come down to two perceptions. The first is how you perceive the enemy, and the second is how you perceive your God. Every victory and every defeat will come down to those two perceptions.

When the Israelites came back after forty years in the wilderness, they had to fight the same giants. They turned to Caleb, who was one of the two spies who said he was ready to fight forty years earlier, and said, "Caleb, are you ready?" He said, "My sword has been drawn for forty years. I've been waiting to fight for forty years. Let's do it. Let's go" (author's paraphrase). Caleb knew the size of his God. He knew the God he served. So his perception of God was clear. And his perception of the enemy was clear.

If you view the enemy in front of you and say, "I can't do it; this is gonna take me out," it will. But if you look at it and say, "My God is bigger than you," now that's a little different.

The second idea is your posture. What is your posture when you're walking through things? Posture does matter. You can't be walking around defeated and falling apart. You can have moments of falling apart, but always be sure to pick yourself up, wash your face, put your head up and your shoulders back. You are a child of the highest God. You can walk with that confidence, strength, and understanding. Walk with victory. Leader, your people are watching you walk.

When you walk through things, there are several types of posture you must have. One is to have a posture of prayer. Teach your people to stop trying to figure out everyone's opinion about what you're going through. Find out one person's opinion and get into the Word of God. Ask God what His opinion is. And like Daniel, may we pray to the God that we serve continuously.

They accused Daniel because he was a man of prayer. And because he was a man of prayer, he was set free. What they thought they were going to trap him with ended up being his way out. Be a woman or a man of prayer. Pray through your things. Don't talk through your things but pray through them. Seek God.

I was on my way with five others to a leader's conference in Alabama a few years back. We got to the airport and found that the flight was canceled because the plane was broken, and they couldn't find another flight for us. We sat there for about an hour and a half trying to figure out our flights again, and then finally, we got on a plane. We were up in the air for fifteen to twenty minutes, and this plane started rocking and rolling.

I have heard many times that turbulence is not dangerous, but I don't believe it. Our plane was suspended in the air, nothing holding it up, and it was shaking like a maraca. Nobody could move from their seat.

Each of us was reading a Bible, a book, or whatever, and then the shaking started getting really bad. I wish someone would have taken a picture because at one time, all five sets of hands went up, and you heard a little bit of prayer coming out of each pastor's mouth. And the plane leveled off just like that. It was so cool.

We will walk through things that will rattle and roll, shake and tremble. But our posture is prayer. Our posture is to lift our hands and our voices before the King of Kings and the Lord of Lords. We led on that plane, and everyone saw our hands raised, heard our prayers, and felt the peace of God. As leaders, our posture is to take the authority God has given us as His children and stand, speak, and declare. Our job is to be filled with the Holy Spirit and to allow His Spirit to pray and move through us.

Another idea is worship. When things get hard, we need to worship. Worship out loud. If that bill comes, sing over the bill. If the medical report comes, sing over the report. Worship is saying that these circumstances are not bigger than the God we serve. When we begin to worship out loud, we get the right perspective. We can also play worship music in our cars or when we sleep. Let our hearts be filled with worship. Sing unto the Lord.

What did the Lord instruct Israel to do again and again before each battle? Worship. You know how many times they worshiped, but they never actually went to battle? By the time they finished worshiping, the enemy had run away. There's power in worship. And we need to take a posture of worship. We need to take a posture of prayer and a posture of faith. Does that mean we always get it right? No. Things will rattle us, but it's okay. We get up, wash our faces, and do it again. Come in with a posture of understanding whose child you are, who you belong to. You belong to the King of Kings and the Lord of Lords. Walk with that posture.

And the third idea is God's promises. Grab hold of the promises of God. Do you know that your God does not lie? If He promised something, then He will bring it to pass. So, you, child of God, need to grab hold of the promises that apply to your circumstance and apply to what you're walking through.

You need to hold them with both hands until things come to pass.

A few years back, I walked through my own difficult thing. I got very sick, and I stayed sick. I was coughing profusely, struggling to breathe. I went to a lot of doctors and was told, "Oh, it's this, or it's that." They put me on pounds of medication, but nothing was working.

Eventually they said they really didn't know what it was, so they sent me to a specialist. After visiting four, five, six specialists, nobody could figure out what was going on. And my coughing and breathing were getting worse. I was getting winded pretty quickly, and going up a flight of stairs made me feel like I had hit a wall.

Then I pulled out my arsenal and began to pray for healing.

But it was not moving, so I prayed again, and I reached out for another arsenal—my family. I'm like, "Hey, need you all to begin to pray for me." I'm like, "Sisters, I need you to pray for me."

I heard back, "We got you."

So now everyone was praying, but still nothing was moving. And I was getting worse. Same as Daniel, my situation was getting worse. I was doing everything I knew to do. Finally, the doctor said, "The x-ray looks terrible. I don't know what this is. We're going to start thinking maybe this is cancer . . ." So we began to search. We began to look. The doctor said, "You know what, we're going to send all your files over to Columbia. They have specialists there; let's see if they can figure it out."

And in the midst of all this, I have to lead because people were watching to see how I lived this out! I began to pray because my posture is prayer. I was not going to sit and worry. I was not going to surf the internet and Google every possible symptom because Google's not my source, Jesus is. So I began to pray. I said, "Lord, what do you want me to do? What's the plan?"

The Lord said, "I want you to read Psalm 91 over yourself each day."

I said, "Okay." I hadn't used that tool yet, but I would use it. I read Psalm 91 out loud each day.

However, I still got worse. Now my hands were turning blue because I was not getting enough oxygen. I couldn't walk from my car to the church or up the stairs in the church without being winded.

But I was just doing what God told me to do. I read His Word each day, and I put my Bible over my blue hands. I would read Psalm 91, sometimes even winded while doing so. I said, "Lord, I believe You. I'm doing all I'm supposed to do. I'm going to doctors, I'm doing it all, but this is my battle plan." And I stayed there eight months. Eight months of reading the promises of God. Eight months of declaring God's Word. Eight months of not seeing anything tangible. Eight months with the doctors now saying, "If you come in again, and your oxygen is this low, we have to admit you to the hospital. We can't send you home." One day as I was reading Psalm 91, I almost passed out. I said out loud, "Devil, I may pass out, but I will get up and finish saying Psalm 91. You won't win!" I never passed out!

And then on March 9, my worst day, I was sitting in my office and I said, "Lord, I don't even know if I can walk down to the car. I don't have the strength. I don't have the breath." And

I began to hear the words of a song in my ear: "It's Your breath in my lungs. It's Your breath in my lungs. It's Your breath in my lungs." That gave me the strength to drive home.

Once I got home and sat on my bed, I began to feel prayers all around me. I said, "Lord, what am I feeling?"

He said, "You're feeling the prayers that you and everybody have been praying for nine months all at one time."

I just began to feel it because prayers have no expiration date. So they now began to lift up all at one time, and Psalm 91 was repeating in my heart, and I fell into a deep sleep. I haven't had a symptom since I woke up on March 10. I was completely healed because His Word is true, and His promises are true.

Leader, God has promises for you. Grab hold of them for you and your people. Grab hold of them with both hands. If you have experienced months of reading the Word and seeing no difference, that doesn't matter. God's all about the subtleties, and all He requires is for you to grab hold of His Word.

You've been granted victory, child of God, so it's your job to grab hold of His promises with both hands and say, "I'm holding here until You produce Your perfect will in my life." So today I pray that as you lead with courage holding onto key principles and trusting the beauty of the process of leadership, that the Word of God challenges you.

When we walk through the processes of our lives, our perception, posture, and holding to the promises of God will allow our leaderships to be beautiful because God's at the front. Leaders, we must live the beauty of the process with courage and display it well for those coming up behind us!

CHAPTER TEN

Being a Courageous Game Changer

I BELIEVE GOD WANTED me to cap this book with this phrase: "You are a game changer." I hope to infuse that into each leader who reads this book. You are a leader, a game changer with the courage to lead. Some of you might say, "Well, she's not talking about me. I'm not a game changer." But I want to tell you that this phrase applies to each leader. You *are* a game changer.

Before the Lord Jesus Christ was arrested in the Garden, He prayed a famous prayer. Some call it the John 17 prayer (paraphrased in the paragraphs below). John 17 is like Jesus's epitaph, the synopsis of His ministry. This prayer to His Father is broken into three parts: Jesus's prayer for Himself, for His disciples, and for His disciples yet to come. The disciples yet to come are you and me.

Isn't it beautiful that Jesus prayed for us before we ever began to serve Him? And He prayed this beautiful prayer right before He was arrested, right before He was beaten, right before He was crucified. He first prayed for Himself, and He said, "Father I know that my time on earth is coming to an end. I know You're going to take me home soon. I thank You that You've given me all authority while I was here."

Then He went on to say, "I have finished all that you've put in front of me. All that I was supposed to do, I did." What an incredible statement. All that God the Father wanted Him to do, he did. May each of us be able to say those same words! Then Jesus began to pray for the disciples and for us. He said, "Now, Lord God, I've given them, the ones you've entrusted to me, everything they need." What has He given us? We lack nothing because Jesus has given us everything we need.

"Now, Father," He continued, "I've also given them your Word. Take that Word and sanctify them with it. Sanctify them with that Word." Then He said, "I don't pray that you take them out of the world, but I pray that you keep them from the evil one." He makes an incredible statement when He says, "As you sent me into the world, I now send them." Just as Jesus was sent into the world and then removed, now He sends us.

How does He send us? Well, He certainly doesn't send us just to survive the world. He certainly doesn't send us just to endure it. Is it possible that Jesus sent us into the world to change it, leader? Is it possible that God has sent the church into the world to change the world? That's absolutely the reason. Does Jesus really expect us to change the world? Yes, because Jesus Himself was a game changer.

Everywhere Jesus went, the circumstance changed. Everywhere Jesus was present, there was healing. There was deliverance. There was power. There was hope. Everywhere He went, the Kingdom of God was advanced. We could say, "Well, that's Jesus. He is the King of Kings, and He is the Lord of Lords. He is the Messiah." Yet Jesus stepped out of Heaven and became like man. What does that mean? He was hungry. He was tired. He was lonely. He was rejected. He was betrayed. He was mistreated. He was abused. He cried. Does that sound familiar to you, leader?

Jesus became like us to show us how to become like Him. He became like us and walked our steps to say, "Hey, I did it. You can do it." He became our trailblazer. He set an example for the path. He said, "I walked holy. You can walk holy. I've walked righteously. You can walk righteously. I've walked under the power of the Holy Spirit. So can you. I did it. I can lead all those whom the Lord has entrusted to me. So can you."

His goal for coming to Earth was to save us 1,000 percent, but He also trail-blazed the way for us to lead others. The way Jesus walked on Earth was the way He is asking His church to walk. He walked into circumstances and situations and was the game changer—He expects us to do the same. He said, "I've given you all you need. *You lack nothing!*" The way He led is the way He wants us to lead—with courage, confidence, and power. He knew the way, He showed the way, and He led the way. Leader, you lack nothing because Jesus has shown you the way. The path is clear for us to follow courageously and do the same.

Three Distinct Marks of a Game-Changing Leader

Jesus had three distinct markers in His life that made Him a game-changing leader. The first marker was that He was filled with the power of the Holy Spirit. Jesus's life was marked with power. He truly moved in the power of the Holy Spirit. We only have a few of His miracles in the Bible, but there were many more. He healed the sick, opened blind eyes, raised the dead, and restored life completely. Not only that, but the Holy Spirit empowered Him to teach and minister to the people effectively. Many times, the Bible indicates that Jesus knew what was in the thoughts and hearts of the people to whom He ministered. How did He know? The Holy Spirit empowered Him. He was able to answer questions that were set up to trap Him with unbelievable wisdom. How? With the power of the Holy Spirit. And the Bible is clear: the Holy Spirit will empower us as leaders today also. One of the reasons we lack nothing is because we have the Holy Spirit. We can lean on Him, be empowered by Him, and be sanctified through Him

The second marker is that Jesus was sanctified by the Word of God. He lived right. Not only did Jesus constantly quote the Scripture, He lived them. In Luke 4 we have the story of the devil trying to tempt Jesus in the wilderness, and the only weapon Jesus used was the Word of God. Nothing else. Not only did Jesus use it as a weapon against the devil, He used it as the measuring stick for His life. Jesus made sure His life and the Word agreed. Jesus Himself set the example for holy living; He was human but did not sin. He allowed the Word of God to be His standard and governed His life with it. Every leader should live this way. The Word of God in the life of a leader is without compromise; it must be the standard. Everything in our leadership must be submitted and surrendered to the Word.

The third marker is that Jesus was in constant communication with the Father. He would spend all night in prayer talking to the Father. Jesus talked to the Father before many major decisions. He would cry out to Him and worship Him. His communication with the Father was always fluid with no ending. By investing time in prayer and seeking the Father's will, Jesus reaped the reward of always knowing God's heart. Any leader who wants to know the heart of God must invest in spending time with Him. You can't know His heart without investing time.

Those three markers made Jesus a game-changing leader, and those three together will make you a game-changing leader as well. You're filled with the power of the Holy Spirit. You're allowing the Word of God to sanctify your life, and you're in communication with the Father. You become who God has called you to be. You become a game changer and lead with courage.

You Can Lead with Courage

I believe there is another quality Jesus possessed as a leader that we need in order to lead courageously and be game changers. It is meekness. Let me illustrate with verses found in Acts 3:1–10:

> Now Peter and John went up together to the temple at the hour of prayer, the ninth hour. And a certain man, lame from his mother's womb, was carried, who they laid daily at the gate of the temple, which is called Beautiful, to ask alms, from those who entered the temple; who, seeing Peter and John about to go into the temple, asked them for alms.

And fixing his eyes on them, with John, Peter said, "Look at us." So he gave them his attention, expecting to receive something from them. Then Peter said, "Silver and gold I do not have, but what I do have I give you: In the name of Jesus Christ of Nazareth, rise up and walk." And he took him by the right hand and lifted him up, and immediately his feet and ankle bones received strength. So he, leaping up, stood and walked and entered the temple with them, walking, leaping and praising God. And all the people saw him walking and praising God. Then they knew that it was him was sat begging alms at the Beautiful gate of the temple; and they were filled with wonder and amazement at what had just happened to him.

Here are two leaders of the church who had walked their lives with Jesus. Jesus was gone. They've had the day of Pentecost, so now they were filled with the Holy Spirit, and I love Peter because he was like us. Peter was the fleshiest leader there is. He shoots off his mouth when he shouldn't. He couldn't back up what he said. He had anger issues. He drew swords and cut off people's ears. Peter was a mess, but Peter gives me a lot of hope.

So Peter was touched by the power of the Holy Spirit. Peter preached his first message and has a preacher's dream because three thousand people were saved after his first message.

Yet, he was just living his life, filled with the power of the Holy Spirit, understanding who he is in God, knowing the authority he has as a son of God. Afterward, he was walking with John. They're just going to church, to the regular hour of prayer.

As Peter was living his life, he came up to the temple. There was this man who had been lame since birth. Perhaps he was in his thirties or forties. He was born this way, and he had never walked in his life. He didn't know what it felt like to walk. And there was nothing in his heart that would expect something different to happen.

The people who knew him didn't expect something different because the Bible said they laid him at the gate daily. That was his lot—lying down in life. He was the temple beggar.

But Peter and John came upon him, in their daily life, filled with the power of the Holy Spirit, sanctified by the Word, and in communication with the Father. The beggar asked for money, but Peter's answer was: "Silver and gold I do not have, but what I do have . . ." The connection here is because I have all I need, we can marry that to John 17 when Jesus says they have everything thing they need. What I do have, as Peter says, "I give you. In the name of Jesus Christ of Nazareth, rise up and walk" (Acts 3:6). He stretched out his hand, and Peter pulled the man up.

A man who's never walked wouldn't be able to walk right away, but this lame man began to jump, leap, and praise God. His strength was completely restored, and he was completely healed. That's Jesus on display. That's what meekness looks like.

Then the man went in the temple and everybody began to praise God. They learned that Jesus of Nazareth had touched him, healed him. Jesus, the person they had crucified.

Then Peter and John were arrested and brought before the Sanhedrin. They were rebuked, but the Sanhedrin, as the Bible says in Acts 4:13, marveled at Peter and John because the two were uneducated and unschooled men, yet they resembled Jesus.

They looked like Him, they smelled like Him, and they talked like Him because Jesus came here to teach us how to become like Him; they watched Him, and they learned. They were filled with the Spirit, so when they showed Jesus on display, those around them didn't see Peter and John. They saw Jesus. The Kingdom was advanced that day. That example of Peter and John should be seen in us. Their meekness displayed the power of God clearly and concisely.

As Christians, we misunderstand the word *meek*. Meek doesn't mean quiet and reserved. Meek means power under control. People who are meek are not powerless. They just know how to walk in confidence. Yet the church has taken on this mousy approach to meekness. For example, we say we don't want to bother anybody, but we will live a good little Christian life and tell people, "God bless you" when the opportunity comes up, and "I'm praying for you." And we think that those kinds of responses represent the meekness of the church on display. But the church was meant to be a bold, powerful presentation of the Kingdom of Jesus Christ. We were meant to put God on display. We were meant to be bold. We were meant to be ferocious.

Let me illustrate with a personal example. I was on a cruise vacation with a great friend of mine. We had gotten off the boat in Jamaica and were looking at jewelry. As I stood there, I saw a woman and her husband from the cruise ship. Attendants were passing around drinks on a glass tray, and they accidently dropped the glass tray on the woman's foot, and she was all cut up. She was bleeding everywhere. The store attendants panicked.

One man grabbed all these dirty rags and put them on her bloody leg.

I watched for about three minutes before I stopped them. I asked what the lady's name was, and she said Alice. I said, "Alice, sit down right here." I brought up her leg and put a napkin on it.

The woman in charge of the store said, "Oh, oh, everybody, listen to her. She's a nurse."

I decided to roll with that!

I cleaned Alice's leg.

She leaned over and asked if I was a nurse.

I said, "No. It's okay. I know what I'm doing, though."

As I was cleaning her leg, I said I was so sorry this had happened. She said that this is the worst vacation of her life. She said, "This happened today, and last night I choked in the dining room, and no one came to help me. My husband had to do the Heimlich maneuver on me. I turned blue for a minute." Her husband was standing there; he was in his seventies as well. He was crying—he was not even speaking. He was just beside himself.

I look at them both and said, "But Alice, it's okay."

"What do you mean?"

"Right now, I'm in the store with you because God wants to remind you that He loves you and that He has a plan for you. This was not by chance or a coincidence that I'm here. I'm going to pray for you, and this situation is now going to change."

Her eyes got big, and she just stared at me.

The friend who was with me, who also understands that she's a game changer, said, "All right, let's pray." So she lifted her hands and prayed.

I put my hand on Alice and her husband, and I began to pray out loud. The whole store prayed. Everyone just kind of nodded their heads and prayed for Alice.

I gave Alice a kiss on the cheek and said, "I'll see you later, Alice. You're going to be fine."

About an hour and a half later, I saw her walking around shopping. I said, "How you doing?"

She said, "It's okay. I think the bleeding stopped. I think I'm all right. But," she said, "I need to know where you girls are because I need my prayer team close; I don't know if this is turned around yet."

I said, "Well, we're close. We're on the same boat. Relax."

Three days later, I saw Alice on the last day of the cruise, walking around the boat. I said, "Alice. How are you?"

She said, "This has been the best vacation of my life."

What is that? That's God on display. Alice is not going to remember me. She's not going to remember my friend. She's going to remember that Jesus showed up in that store and met her and changed the circumstance for her.

We've been called to flip impossible circumstances. We've been called to be faithful and to be bold and to be humble. We don't know what's really going to happen when we step out to serve, but that's really none of our business. It's God's business. We're not the divine healer. We're not the divine deliverer. We're simply the humble facilitator, called to lead like Jesus led.

As we go forth, speaking in boldness, creating a pocket for God to move, we know that if God chooses not to heal, not to work in someone's life immediately, or He chooses to do something different in that circumstance, that's God. We are just vessels God can use.

You might be at the end of this book about leading with courage saying, "Well, that's great, but I don't have that kind of courage." If you're a leader, you have the empowering choice to ask for boldness, to ask for faith, to ask for humility, to ask for courage. We misunderstand and think courage is the absence of fear, but it's not. Courage is moving in the midst of fear. We are fully human with all the natural frailties of the flesh, but if we pray and ask God for whatever we are lacking, He will give it to us. All we need to do is ask in faith, trusting God to equip us and to work in and through us.

Our constant communication with God allows us to be game changers, leaders influencing others for Christ. As we are in constant prayer, God is working constantly using the Word in our lives to sanctify us. We are filled with the Spirit, which allows us to be game changers, and then when we walk into our schools, our jobs, or any place, we become catalysts of change, catalysts of hope, catalysts of deliverance, catalysts of healing.

You become a catalyst of all these things, and no matter where you lead, everyone will know you are a child of God. People will ask you to pray for them because they know where hope is. They know where power is. That's who you have to be, leader. In this hour, in this time, you have to be that game changer. You have to be filled with the Holy Spirit, sanctified by His Word, dwelling in communication with the Father, which will allow you to put God on display. The Bible says that if He is lifted up, He will draw all men unto Him. It's not necessarily our job to draw out, but it's our job to lift Jesus up, so He can work through us to work in others' lives. To live and lead with courage, we live and lead with authority. We might be afraid of the word *authority*, but we don't have to be because we're children of God. God gave us authority to pray with authority and to speak with authority. He gives us authority. *Walk in it!*

May we understand that the race is not given to the swift nor the battle to the strong, but it's given to him who endures to the end. May we understand that we are in a race, and we are moving, no matter what we see. May we desire to be found faithful, so that our lives will leave a legacy for those who come behind us. As we pray and lead with authority, we must remember that healing is not our business. Our business is to pray. Our business is to quote the Word. Our business is to live the life. Our job is to lead the way that Jesus led. Leader, you are called to lead with courage so you can be a game changer and change the world for His glory. Have I not commanded you to be strong and of good courage! Courage is not an option it's a commitment! Go and lead courageously!

Order Information

To order additional copies of this book, please visit
www.redemption-press.com.
Also available on Amazon.com, BarnesandNoble.com, and
MarshaMansour.com
Or by calling toll free 1-844-2REDEEM.

CPSIA information can be obtained
at www.ICGtesting.com
Printed in the USA
FSHW021717180519